T0166743

PENGUIN BOOKS

THE ASIAN MAVERICK

Chris Lee is an entrepreneur, investor, startup advisor, and senior executive in the healthcare industry with extensive international experience. He is one of the few Asians to rise to the global executive committee level in two Fortune 500 healthcare companies, with a strong track record in business growth, M&A, new market expansion, and innovation incubation.

Chris grew up in Korea and Japan, and started his career as a medical sales representative in the US, eventually working in more than ten countries across three continents. He was appointed country manager of Bristol-Myers Squibb at the age of thirty and became the first-ever executive committee member of Asian descent in Bayer's 150-year history at age thirty-nine. Chris has deep and extensive healthcare experience, having managed businesses across various healthcare segments in the last three decades, including pharmaceuticals, medical devices, diagnostics, consumer health, animal health, and more.

In 2022, Chris founded VentureBlick, an international fundraising platform matching healthcare startups and medical investors. He aims to transform the healthcare fundraising building on his years of accumulated industry experience and professional network.

Chris is an advocate of inclusive leadership and workplace happiness. He wrote two bestselling books, *Emotional Management* and *Marketing Works*. He regularly contributes leadership articles to *Forbes* and actively shares his personal learnings on LinkedIn. He has won multiple leadership awards, including 'Most Respected CEO' for three consecutive years (2020–2022) by Great Place to Work, and 'Executive of the Year 2021' by *Singapore Business Review*.

Notes From Members of Staff

Australia:

'Dear Chris, we first met at the FY19 President's Club held in London. This was such a memorable event that you and your team of professionals organized. We were all treated too well with much generosity. Thank you. I wish you every success and happiness for your future endeavours.'

Japan:

'Thank you Chris-san. I felt that you are very charismatic, instantly understanding the nuances of Japan and delivering messages that motivated everyone. Thank you for giving a very warm message to our employees in Japan in the video of the latest Japan Town Hall. I remembered many engaged initiatives by you and felt your thoughts for Japan. Please come to Tokyo again!'

'Dear Chris-san, I strongly feel that no other leader has implemented measures that all employees have enjoyed as much as Chris-san has. From leaving work early on Fridays, to distributing DEMAECAN coupons, to free vending machines and the cafe, to distributing goodies during the transition to telework, etc. Thank you from the bottom of my heart. It is truly regrettable that you are leaving the company, but I wish you all the best in your future endeavours.'

'Do you remember your first face-to-face town hall in Japan? I clearly remember you kept emphasising your passion to improve OHS from the bottom #14 to the world class. To be honest, I was a little bit doubtful at that time as 'Japan discount' has been used as an excuse in the past many years. But you have led us to achieving the 'mission impossible' goal! We became to believe 'Yes, we can' under your leadership, we will definitely miss you as an inspiring leader! Thank you for all of the innovative changes you have brought to APAC! All the best for your new endeavour!'

Korea:

'Hello Mr Chris, looking at the boss who always works hard for his employees, I've been thinking a lot about how lucky I am to have a happy working life. Although I can't talk much with the boss while living in the company, I haven't been able to say thank you very much, but it's a pity that I'm finally able to say thank you. I sincerely hope that you are always healthy and happy. Thank you!'

'Dear Chris, 크리스 사장님, I really wanted to thank you and wish you all the best. I've never met a leader like you—you were one of a kind, unique, well-respected, much-loved president for all. With the learning, open, respectful culture you introduced, I was able to meet many wonderful colleagues and to challenge myself via cross-border transfer (Korea and Japan). Thank you so much. I will always remember you as the leader who gave me a handwritten card for congratulating me for my wedding, and I will constantly check your status via LinkedIn. 제가 메드트로닉과 함께한 3년은 크리스 사장님과 함께여서 즐거웠고, 감사했고, 배움이 많았고, 늘 새로웠습니다. Thank you and stay healthy. Hope I can meet you in the future again!'

'Boss, I'm not very talkative, so I couldn't express it when I met you in person I boasted a lot, saying that there is no boss like this to the people around me! Haha! Out of all of my company life so far, the past three years have been the happiest time for me, and I am grateful for making such a time. It will! And

I must have seen the CEO the most in our company. Especially on screen! That's why I think I heard more affection. Please continue to maintain that great look in the future~!! :)'

Singapore:
'Thank you for all that you did for APAC employees! I especially enjoyed the talks you provided to employees in Singapore. I learnt so much from these talks and even shared some of the key learnings with my team. Enjoy the break before your next role and hope our paths will cross soon. Wishing you all the very best!'

'Dear Chris, on many occasions where we have leadership team meetings, lunch, or other events, I enjoyed it a lot whenever you shared your personal experiences, vision on equality and on bringing Asians to leadership roles. You are truly inspirational! Through your leadership, we break away from the stereotype and I admire how much you care about talent development, which has influenced me to lead that way as well. All the best to you and looking forward to your vlog/LinkedIn updates!'

'Dear Chris, thanks so much for the leadership and welfare that you have given to the staff. We appreciate it a lot, especially the 4.5-days work week and December holidays! It really motivates us to push even further and improve our efficiency. Under your leadership, more people know about Service and Repair now and the work we do. Thanks once again, take care and all the best in your future endeavours!'

'Dear Chris, you are definitely a president who stood out (in a good way)! Not just for the benefits and free food that was offered during your time here in APAC. We could all see the genuine care and concern you have for employees and even their family. You have no qualms of wearing interesting costumes or putting up a performance because you wanted employees to also have a good time during the townhalls. Perhaps, I don't say this enough when I see you around in the MBC office but here is one last big THANK YOU!! Take care and all the best!'

'When I discuss Medtronic with my family, you are one of my favourite topics. Your leadership, your presentation, your generosity, your sense of humour . . . too many things I can share with my family that I have a great leader to be proud of. Because of you, I never want to miss any town hall even though I am on leave. Because of you, I am inspired to engineer the extraordinary.'

'Dear 사장님,
Thank you for always listening to us and your utmost support to drive 'inclusion and diversity'. Love your sense of humour in townhalls. You are an amazing leader who supported our very first Medtronic Muslims and Friend's (MMF) charity fundraising. I enjoyed and appreciated all your various initiatives for the wellness of our employees. You made Medtronic a great place to work. We will miss you. Best of luck for your next move ♥. 감사합니다!'

Taiwan:

'Thank you for your great leadership in the past ten years for GC and APAC. You may not know me well, but I was in Medtronic Greater China when you were the Greater China leader, then you moved to APAC leader and I was lucky to be the first person who moved to Australia under the Talent-X program. I truly appreciate all the opportunities/initiatives you have created for Medtronic employees, to allow them to continue to develop their careers. I wish you all the best and you will be missed by all of us!'

The Philippines:

'Thank you, Chris, for your leadership! YOU are the BEST. I am very grateful to have a leader who always takes care of their people no matter what the position is in the company. We are always fond of taking pictures with you during any event. I valued your honesty and sincerity in every town hall or anytime I hear you speak. All the BEST for your future, may God continue to bless you and your family! We will miss you here in APAC.'

USA:

'Chris, I didn't get to witness the hard work that went into it, but I definitely enjoyed being a part of a strong business with a wonderful work culture which you created. I can say, however, that I will remember a leader who followed through on his word; a leader who valued his employees, a leader who was innovative in his execution. Thank you for your forward vision, approachable personality, and humour.'

The Asian Maverick

Chris Lee

PENGUIN BOOKS
An imprint of Penguin Random House

PENGUIN BOOKS

USA | Canada | UK | Ireland | Australia
New Zealand | India | South Africa | China | Southeast Asia

Penguin Books is part of the Penguin Random House group of companies
whose addresses can be found at global.penguinrandomhouse.com

Published by Penguin Random House SEA Pte Ltd
9, Changi South Street 3, Level 08-01,
Singapore 486361

First published in Penguin Books by Penguin Random House SEA 2023
Copyright © Chris Lee 2023

10 9 8 7 6 5 4 3 2 1

The views and opinions expressed in this book are the author's own and the
facts are as reported by him which have been verified to the extent possible,
and the publishers are not in any way liable for the same.

ISBN 9789815127102

Typeset in Adobe Caslon Pro by MAP Systems, Bengaluru, India

www.penguin.sg

Contents

Foreword

'Chris, why are you writing a third book?', many have asked. There isn't a singular answer, but many reasons snowballing into this vision. I've written two books before this one. The first was about marketing, while the second was about emotional management.

The idea of writing the third book didn't cross my mind until I had reached corporate retirement age. I've had a long and storied career, and many of my peers were already kicking back with daiquiris on the beaches around the world. But I didn't feel like stopping just yet. Like in sports, there are still seconds left on the clock to make one more great play in life.

That great play is not this book. It's my new company VentureBlick. But I wanted to encapsulate all the lessons I had learned leading global organizations into a tome, explain my reasons for my belief that Asian leadership sensibilities is much needed in this day and age, and encourage you, yes, you, the reader, that age should never be a barrier to achieving something great.

There is an oft-repeated saying, 'Be wary of an old man in a profession where men usually die young.' Entrepreneurship is a young man's game, but there's still some life in me yet.

If this was a typical book on leadership, this foreword would be written by a senior leader who has contributed immensely to my development. But this is not just any book. It's about being an Asian maverick and standing out from the crowd, using leadership examples that you'd rarely see in other companies. My three decades in multiple corporations have taught me that managing down is just as, if not more, important than managing up. If you take only one leadership philosophy from this book, let it be that.

In this spirit, I've included several comments, edited for length and clarity, from my former employees. I haven't personally met some of them, but I'm glad that my work has made such an impact on their lives. To kick it off, the first comment is from one of my former bosses, and someone I admire a lot, who made a huge impact on my career and shaped my leadership style.

Enjoy the book.

* * *

How to Read This Book

Most self-help books allow you to jump between different chapters, depending on your interest in a topic. I'd highly recommend that you read *The Asian Maverick* chronologically instead. I've always believed that the best lessons are told through stories, shared while toasting marshmallows over a crackling campfire or during mealtimes with phones kept aside.

We remember not to fly too close to the sun lest we fall into the sea like Icarus (although this really is a story about using the right tools for the job; wax is a terrible bonding agent for feathers).

We are familiar with the two wolves that live inside us, usually erroneously attributed to Native Americans. One spreads hope, love, and positivity, while the other wolf is darkness, despair, and negativity. Both wolves are in eternal combat with each other. We know that the wolf that wins is 'the one we feed'.

We remember lessons and concepts better when they are told through stories, which is why you'll find many of them littered throughout each chapter. Most of the stories are in chronological order and I regularly make references to earlier chapters in later parts of the book, so you might get confused if you jump around.

But I also understand that not every story—and subsequent lesson—is applicable to you, which is why I've included summaries, cheekily called 'ChrisNotes' (a nod to Cliff Notes), at the start of every chapter.

I'm also a big advocate of journalling as a learning tool, which is why I've also included some questions for you to ponder over at the end of every chapter. I highly encourage you to scribble your answers in the book or to run wild with a highlighter. Dog-ear pages, use bookmarks, or doodle in between the pages of each chapter. We learn better through writing.

You can also share your thoughts with me on LinkedIn. I would love to hear them. As you'll slowly find out over the course of the next eleven chapters, I believe that learning is a two-way street, and there is much I can learn from you, too.

Chapter One

The End and the Beginning

I'd consider the chair in my previous office to be exceedingly comfortable. It's a plush, high-backed leather piece with armrests that end nicely where my wrists start. I'm certain it's a Herman Miller, but my knowledge of furniture brands is rudimentary. But I rarely got to enjoy the chair's creature comforts. I travelled extensively for work—out of the 365 days in the year, I was only in Singapore for 50 to 100 days.

Still, I considered myself blessed. I was the Asia-Pacific President for a large, listed multinational medical technology company, Medtronic, and oversaw close to 10,000 people spread out in sixty locations across multiple countries that include Australia, India, Japan, Korea, Singapore, and more. Globally, it operates in 150 countries and boasts a massive workforce of 100,000.

Medtronic has been around for a long time—electrical engineering student Earl Bakken and his brother-in-law Palmer Hermundslie founded the company in 1949 in a tiny 800-square foot garage after the Second World War. It faced a financially rocky start. In its first month of business, Medtronic only made $8, repairing hospitals' electronic equipment. While its revenue improved incrementally over time, it was nothing to write home about—until 1957.

A young surgeon asked Bakken if he could engineer a pacemaker—a medical device that regulates heart rhythm—that did not need to rely on an external power supply. Bakken built a small, battery-powered device that created the foundation of Medtronic today. Its medical equipment and technology are some of the finest in the industry, and professionals trust the brand. Beyond pacemakers, which the company still produces, it also manufactures several life-saving devices, including stents, insulin pumps, and more. In the fiscal year of 2022, Medtronic reported revenues topping US\$31 billion, cementing its position as the number one medical device company in the world.

Asia-Pacific was a key market. In 2021, it accounted for 13 per cent, or US\$4 billion, of the company's revenues and was growing faster than other regions.

And yet, in spite of these fantastic numbers and my admittedly cushy position at the top, I was getting restless. Honestly, I had no reason to feel this way. I was healthy—or as healthy as I could be since Korean fried chicken always bested me and I spent far too much time in meetings and too little time exercising. I was on the wrong side of fifty and closer to retirement than rambunctiousness. I could have coasted along until it was time to break out my fishing rods and enjoy the fruits of my labour—I had been in the medical and pharmaceutical industry for over three decades, and built an extensive network that I could rely on—in my twilight years.

When people stay still and don't grow, they die. Not physically, of course, but from within. Their souls slowly wither and eventually, their countenance, too. William Wallace, a famous Scottish warrior from the thirteenth century who led his countrymen to victory against the English and whom Mel Gibson played in *Braveheart*, once said, 'Every man dies. Not every man really lives.' I was beginning to feel those deathly tendrils slither their way into my mental state and wanted to snap out of it before it was too late.

The chair, unfortunately, was beginning to feel too comfortable.

* * *

I grew up in a typically conservative South Korean household. My parents were doctors. My father was a surgeon general in the Korean army. When he retired at fifty-four, he opened a private hospital that he slowly nurtured into a success. He ran it until his peaceful passing thirty years later in 2011. My three elder brothers also regularly topped their respective schools. Naturally, my father also expected me to perform well in my studies and become a doctor just like him.

But, I was a terrible student. I kept coming last in school and always had to obscure that knowledge from my father. I preferred hanging out with my friends. I even formed a band. It was called 'Mystery', a play on our names as all of us had the surnames Lee—Mister Lee, hence 'Mystery'. I was the lead singer and drummer. In Japan, where I studied for two years, I formed another band called 'Dreamer'. We played everywhere. My studies naturally suffered.

Every year, seventeen-year-old Korean teenagers would sit through the Suneung, or the College Scholastic Ability Test, to determine if they could enter college. This annual examination is an eight-hour-long ordeal that can potentially shape the life of its takers. The maximum score one can get is 340 and the cut-off score to enter university is 260. I scored in the low 100s.

My plan? Further my studies in the US instead. I convinced my father that I should head there and he agreed. However, the embassy rejected my visa application, probably because they thought that I would overstay and disappear into the weeds. Fortunately, I found an agency specializing in American visas and successfully got one.

This was in the 1980s, a time when Koreans studying in overseas colleges were a rare sight. But my stints in Japan and the US shaped me greatly and made me realize how small we are in the grand scheme of things. Growing up, I kept hearing that Korea's mountain ranges were the most beautiful in the world. When I went to the Rocky Mountains in Colorado for the first time, my jaw dropped at the sheer brilliance.

It's only when you put yourself in uncomfortable positions that you grow as a human. Comfort breeds complacency and weakness, and gives you an extremely limited worldview. Yes, I wasn't a great student. Many have asked me why I never put the effort in school. It took me a while to realize that I did not like being told what to do. I preferred learning through discovery and application. Rote and memorization bored me. The path of the unknown always seduced me with its myriad of possibilities.

I stood up from my chair and left the office. I wanted to buy a cup of coffee and I usually do my best thinking while walking. Entrepreneurship had intrigued me for a long time, but I never found the right problem to solve or the perfect opportunity to do it. Deep down inside, I also knew that there was that small shadow of a fear whispering negativities into my inner ear.

'What if you fail?'

'You're already famous in this industry. Why do you want to head into the unknown?'

'What can you do that hasn't already been done by someone else?'

I thought about my late father. I didn't know it when I was younger, but he played a huge influence in my life. Although I couldn't go to medical school, I gravitated towards the medical and healthcare industry because of him. One of my fondest memories is showing him a video of me leading an annual conference with a large audience of doctors and medical professionals, all of whom were listening to every word I said. That short clip made him jubilant.

On his deathbed, my father's last words to me were, 'Chris, you must always remember your humble beginnings and respect everyone regardless of their words or jobs. Most importantly, you need to remain a human being, no matter how successful you become.'

Being human can mean many things. But as I sipped on my freshly bought coffee, it only meant one thing to me at that moment in my life: being true to myself.

When I returned to the office and sat back on my chair, my mind was made. I would throw caution to the wind and resign from my job. I wasn't thinking about retirement though. Instead, I wanted to start a company.

It was also a way of paying homage to my father, a serendipitous circle of life. My father founded the hospital when he was fifty-four. I was fifty-six and about to become an entrepreneur for the first time in my life. At that time, many thought that he was far too old to start a business, but he still pressed forward with his decision. I'd imagine that I would receive similar negative sentiments.

Throughout my life, as you'll slowly find out over the next several chapters, I made unconventional and contrarian choices for myself, my teams, my divisions, and my companies. At the core of my decision-making process was always my people and how they would be affected.

In fact, a decade ago, when I was forty-six, I had already entertained the thoughts about leaving the industry, having spent twenty years building and leading teams in different companies and countries. The work had worn me down. I was also slightly disillusioned because my career progression had stagnated, in spite of my exceptional performances. At that time, my plan was to resign and head to Vietnam on a fact-finding trip, hoping to spot opportunities and start a company.

But, I joined Medtronic instead.

I didn't want to second-guess myself again. I also wanted to show my peers, my employees, and the people around me that age shouldn't prevent you from pursuing something you've always wanted. My heart firm and my mind calm, I penned my resignation letter and submitted it.

My father ran the hospital for thirty years. I want to achieve the same with my company. I called it VentureBlick, a name derived from three words: venture—to explore and invest in promising businesses; republic—equal opportunities for everyone; blick—to shine, glitter, or gleam (in Old English).[1]

I was excited, like that moment when your heart pauses just before the roller-coaster plunges into a dizzying drop. Many mistake that feeling for fear, but with the right mindset, you can mould it into excitement. Both emotions, after all, activate the same part of your brain—the hypothalamus.

My father always said that if you chase after money, money may not come to you. But if you chase after your dream, money will follow. It may sound a little idealistic, but what it really means to me is that it's more important to follow your heart and take certain risks. I'm not a gambling man, but I wanted to roll the dice one last time.

I abandoned the chair. I didn't need its comfort any longer. It was time for an adventure.

---

[1] The definition of 'venture' is derived from the Cambridge Dictionary, while republic is a state of government where power is held by the people. The definition of 'blick' is from *Wiktionary.org*.

Chapter Two

Who Is Chris Lee?

'A leader is one who sees more than others see, who sees farther than others see, and who sees before others do.'
—John Maxwell, American author and speaker, *The 21 Irrefutable Laws of Leadership*

ChrisNotes

- I grew up in a wealthy family, but had to pay my own way through school, because my father didn't believe in handouts.
- I was raised in a family of doctors and medical professionals. But I couldn't cut it in medical school and had to find my own way.
- I left Korea at a young age to study overseas at a time when this was unheard of. My time in different countries shaped my worldview and unorthodox leadership strategies.

Before I became Chris Lee, I was Lee Hee-Yeol (this double barrelled name is pronounced 'here'), a cheeky boy growing up in Korea. On paper, I was born to a wealthy medical family. Both of my parents were in the medical field and I had many relatives in the trade, too. Naturally, many thought I had a silver spoon in my mouth.

The reality was far different. My father always believed that people should work hard and prove themselves, like he did. He had risen from poverty to make a name for himself in Korea and he believed that his five children should do the same. My parents got separated when I was still a boy, so I was left to my own devices for prolonged periods of my childhood.

While I did have nannies and drivers growing up and always had food on the table, I had to earn money for everything else such as school and my other interests. I never received any allowance from my parents. Instead, since I was twelve, I did multiple odd jobs just to earn my keep. I started by delivering newspapers to houses in the mornings. Then, I realized that I could earn more by also delivering milk at the same time. So, I did that too.

And because I was so familiar with the homes in my area, I also started delivering cards and letters during special occasions like Christmas and other holidays. I suppose I already had an entrepreneurial spirit from a young age.

My three older brothers were model students, unlike me. And because our family had such a long medical heritage, all of us were also expected to become doctors. Of course, I never did.

In the first chapter, I mentioned that I left Korea to study in Japan when I was sixteen, and then moved to the US two years later after performing badly in the Suneung, or the College Scholastic Ability Test.

For the first couple of years in the US, I struggled. I barely understood English and had to put in double the work to attain passing grades. But, unlike my growing up years in Korea, I was more motivated in the US. I suppose it was a combination of being untethered from the crushing weight of expectations and the freedom that the country affords to the people. There wasn't just one way to success. You could be whoever you want in the US and no one would judge.

I even expanded my non-academic interests. In Korea, I had practised taekwondo for over a decade; everyone in the country picked up the martial art as a child. I continued my training in the US. While I was considered mediocre in Korea, I was one of the best in North America. The sport was new back then and there weren't many practitioners, so I excelled.

One day, when I was walking to the dojang, a martial arts studio, to train, I saw a poster at the entrance. The country was sending a taekwondo team to Korea for the 1988 Summer Olympics and was accepting athlete applications. It was the first time Seoul hosted the event. Incidentally, it was also the first time taekwondo appeared in the Olympics, albeit as a demonstration sport instead of being part of the standard medal competition.

I hadn't gone back to my home country in several years. I didn't have the money to buy a plane ticket back, so I thought this was my best chance to return and visit my friends and family. I applied to be part of the team, went through the selection process and got picked, and flew to Korea at the American government's expense.

I got my butt handed to me in the first round, naturally. But I was glad to be back. I caught up with my peers, many of whom hadn't seen me in a long time and wanted to know what I've been up to. The Internet was only a military project at the time; so my friends and family knew nothing about my American adventures, save for the occasional phone calls. They marvelled at my English language capabilities, fretted that I hadn't eaten enough, and pored through all the photos I took when I was overseas.

I even managed to carve out time to helm the deejay decks in the Korean clubs. America was starting to flex its soft culture, thanks to its movies and music, and Korea had begun embracing it. My time in the US meant that I was familiar with American pop and hip-hop music, so I played these for a very receptive crowd. I came back for several nights. It helped to earn some pocket money that I could use to fund my stay in the US. After the Olympics ended, I returned to the US to continue my studies.

I managed to earn enough credits to apply for the University of Arizona. By then, I was proficient enough in English to understand the lecturers and complete my coursework. I graduated in 1988. Then, I got into the Thunderbird School of Global Management for the two-year Master's degree programme.

I was pushing hard in my studies, an admittedly stark reversal from my earlier school-going years. Being alone energized me. I didn't have to answer to anyone and could live on my own terms. Some thrive on structure; I preferred a life without guardrails. When I was growing up in Korea, I felt like I was working hard for others. In the US, I had the freedom to express myself and decide who I wanted to be. The country also showed me that there were different routes to success if I was willing to work hard.

My American sojourn imbued a desire within me to travel the world. I didn't want to make memories; I wanted to learn from other cultures. I didn't know it back then, but my passport formed my worldview. As globalization made the world smaller, an increased appreciation for the nuances of other countries became a valuable skill.

Looking back, if I was honest with myself, I also wanted to make my father proud. He was a typical Asian parent, stingy with compliments and praise, and showed his pleasure (or displeasure) through a blend of monosyllabic answers, grunts, and facial expressions. But he shaped me to be the man and leader I am today. In many ways, he is responsible for imbuing the spirit of the Asian maverick within me.

My time in school also made an excellent springboard into the depths of the corporate world, even if I didn't know it back then.

From Classrooms to the Corporate World

MSD (1989–1996)

Even though I couldn't become a doctor, I still wanted to honour my father and be part of the healthcare industry. So, in June 1990, after graduation, I joined Merck, also known as MSD outside of the US. It was the world's biggest pharmaceutical company at that time and had been awarded the 'World's Most Admired Company' by *Fortune* magazine seven years in a row. I started as a management associate in the hopes that I would eventually manage a team one day. Instead, the company asked me to sell its products. I asked for a reason. I thought I had been misled by the job description.

My manager told me, 'Every new employee in MSD must go through the frontlines first and sell, regardless of their role. Even our president started out as a salesperson.' I wasn't happy at first. In Korea, at that point in time, salespeople were not highly regarded. Many had the perception that only those who didn't study hard enough or did badly in school went into sales. They had no other viable career options. When I asked my manager how long I needed to be in sales, he gave a vague answer. 'A year? Ten years? If your sales performance is bad, you should continue being in the field.'

I almost quit on the spot. But I thought about it and gave it a shot. They were the most admired company for a reason.

Looking around the office, I saw doctors and pharmacists slogging alongside management associates like me and scientists with smiles on their faces.

My father, unsurprisingly, wasn't proud of my job. He was disappointed that I didn't become a doctor like him. However, I met doctors every day to sell medical supplies.

Within a year, thanks to a sales and business strategy that no one thought of (I talk about it in length in Chapter Four), I became the top salesperson in the company after spending several weeks firmly at the bottom as the worst performer.

Impressed by my achievement and my ability to negotiate with other business entities, the company posted me to Hong Kong to become the business development manager. Most in MSD take between five and seven years to be promoted to a managerial position. It took me a year. I grabbed this opportunity with both hands. My objective was simple: growing the business in the twelve countries under me by understanding the different markets, identifying potential targets for mergers and acquisitions, and establishing new ones. During my time in the role, I expanded MSD's footprint in Asia and even made inroads into China.

From there, I rapidly rose through the ranks of the company and received promotions almost every year. I was even entrusted to open and lead the Korean subsidiary. The year was 1992 and the country was experiencing strong winds of change. The global pharmaceutical industry recognized Korea as an important market and the political situation was going through tumult, with leaders from three different factions and ideologies battling to win the elections. The Cold War had officially ended and free market democracy had emerged victorious. The world was putting a lot of pressure on countries such as Korea to join the world stage and welcome global trade. I thought it was a great time for me to return to my home country and establish the subsidiary.

While I was given the title of strategic planning director, I essentially headed Korea. It took me about six months to work the ground and review the market. Eventually, after my presentation, I obtained permission to set up a branch office with a paid-up capital of US$10 million. I started MSD Korea. My youth and global experience meant that I was willing to try strategies some might consider brash. But I believed that Korea was ripe for change and would reward bold tactics. Today, it has become one of the largest multinational pharmaceutical companies in the country.

Soon after, I became part of their senior management and then finally rose to the position of director-in-charge of Far East Asia within four years of joining MSD. It was unheard of at that time. I was only twenty-nine and the company's youngest senior executive. I was also the only Asian at that level.

BRISTOL-MYERS SQUIBB (1996–2004)

Even after this corporate success, my father still disapproved of my job. It wasn't his fault. I never fully explained my role to him. He still thought I was selling medical and pharmaceutical supplies to doctors. It was only after he realized that I led multiple countries and had teams of doctors working under me to conduct R&D and sell products that saved people's lives did he understand how important my work was to society.

Eight years after I joined MSD, he finally gave his blessings. By that time, in 1997, I had already left the company after being headhunted to join another firm in the same field— Bristol-Myers Squibb (BMS), as president of the Korean subsidiary.

When I left MSD, 191 employees out of 193 employees under me asked if they could follow me to BMS. These votes of confidence heartened me and showed that my style of leadership was not only effective for business, but people as well.

I remained at BMS for eight years and once again, proved my leadership mettle. My Asian collectivist sensibilities coupled with an understanding of Western organizational culture proved to be a boon. My staff responded to my emotional leadership overtures, which I had refined over time, while the senior executives believed in my vision.

When I turned thirty-six in 2001, the company made me president of Oceania. I was responsible for Australia, New Zealand and the Pacific Islands. The region had over 1,000 employees and was worth almost a billion dollars. I continued working hard and making a name for myself, convinced that I could eventually climb up the ladder and become the CEO of a large global pharmaceutical company. It did look like I was on the way there. German-based conglomerate Bayer poached me in 2005 to lead its Chinese division.

BAYER (2005–2012)

China was a hard nut to crack. Most global companies didn't consider the country an important market at that point in time and only installed small satellite offices. I thought otherwise. The economic reports in 2005 portended China's potential explosive growth. Its exports were growing exponentially in tandem with its gross domestic product numbers and the middle class was expanding rapidly. [1]

After leading the company to the top of the leader board in the country (yet again, using another business strategy I devised that I describe in detail in Chapter Four), I was finally given the opportunity to lead the Asia-Pacific region in 2007. It was a position I had been hankering for a long time.

While it might not seem like a tremendous achievement now, back then, it was rare to see Asians in a senior executive leadership role. Europe- and America-based conglomerates usually post a Western person to lead the Asia-Pacific region. I had never seen an Asian leader become top dog in our part of the world, let alone in regions such as Europe, Africa, or even America.

It made me feel like I finally broke an invisible glass ceiling for all Asians, that we can become leaders of large companies if we worked hard and showed our potential. I continued applying myself at Bayer, but my progress seemed to have stagnated, no matter what I did or the success I achieved.

MEDTRONIC (2012–2022)

I became slightly disillusioned. Then, Medtronic reached out to me, offering me the opportunity to lead its fastest-growing market, China. Initially, I was reluctant to take it. Entrepreneurship had been calling out to me and I thought I could do a lot better leading my own company. I was finally convinced into the role after the then CEO of Medtronic replied, 'Why not?' to my question. I had asked him, 'Will I have the chance to take over your position one day?'

The role wasn't new to me. By that point, I was familiar with all the markets in Asia-Pacific. The demands of the role didn't faze me. I understood the business strategies needed to grow the different regions that came under my purview. I led China for just slightly more than five years, then took over the Asia-Pacific portfolio.

My ambition of becoming the global CEO of a major corporation, however, remained out of reach, no matter how hard I worked and how big the markets I managed grew.

So, after a decade, I left Medtronic. I didn't achieve my ambition, but I was no longer disillusioned. I had done my utmost best in everything I did. My progress up the corporate ranks—and extended plateau—wasn't a reflection of my ability, but a combination of bad luck and ill-timing.

I wasn't ready for retirement though. I still had some fuel left in the tank and wanted to finally take that plunge into entrepreneurship with VentureBlick. The corporate world had sharpened my leadership skills and I believed that I could once again build something from nothing, just like I had done in the past three decades when I carved out a niche for myself in the pharmaceutical industry as the Asian maverick.

But what is a maverick? And how did I build that reputation? It took several decades of hard work and bold actions, some of which could have backfired spectacularly in my face.

* * *

Questions to Ponder Over

1. I've shared who I am with you. Now, do you know who you are? How do you think your friends would describe you in three words?
2. How do you want people to see you? What are the actions you are taking to build that reputation?

Chapter Three

The Maverick Way of Thinking

'A leader takes people where they want to go. A great leader takes people where they don't necessarily want to go, but ought to be.'

—Rosalynn Carter, Former First Lady of the United States, Goodreads.com

---

ChrisNotes

- Doing the same thing repeatedly, yet expecting different results is the definition of insanity. Instead, be bold.
- It might be cliché, but it rings true in the business world. Your actions speak a lot louder than words and don't be afraid to speak out.
- There are bosses and there are leaders. The former stay in the comfort of their throne and bark orders. The latter are remembered and adored.

'What the hell is a maverick?' I remembered thinking to myself. The year was 2004 and I was in conversation with a recruiter about a role in a leading pharmaceutical company.

The then CEO had asked him to find somebody with a 'maverick attitude' to lead Asia-Pacific. The headhunter sent out several feelers and all of them came back with one name: mine.

I never told the recruiter I didn't know the word's meaning. Instead, I nodded my head, pretending to understand. Then I went home to look it up in the Cambridge dictionary.

maverick *noun*

'mæv.ər.ɪk

a person who thinks and acts in an independent way, often behaving differently from the expected or usual way

That got me thinking: would I describe myself as a 'maverick'?

In many ways, I suppose I am. I was the youngest director at Merck, promoted to the role when I was twenty-seven. Two years later, I became its youngest country manager. When I turned thirty-nine, Bayer Healthcare made me the head (senior vice president) for the Asia-Pacific region. I was the first and only Asian in a top global leadership position in the German company.

My career achievements would not have been possible if I stayed in my own lane and applied time-and-tested, historical methods. Following the road that others had trodden on will lead to known outcomes that you might not necessarily want. After all, insanity is doing the same thing multiple times expecting different results.

I've always believed that going against the grain might have higher risks, but exponentially larger pay offs. I have constantly applied my maverick ideals in multiple situations in my career and benefited immensely.

In the next several pages, I'll be sharing four overarching maverick mantras that I always go back to whenever I have to make a difficult decision. They have served me well. I hope they do the same for you, too.

When Everyone Goes Left, Consider Going Right

Twenty years ago, as the first Asian in a global healthcare company leading Australia, I had two options: lead the Japanese division of a company that generated $2 billion in revenue and hired 3,000 employees or take a pay cut and lead a smaller firm in China. Most would opt for the former, but I decided to go for the latter instead. My decision surprised many industry insiders. Some even asked if something bad had happened in my previous role.

The truth was simpler. I wanted to challenge myself and see if I could make a difference for the company in China. I already knew what to expect if I had gone for the bigger pay cheque. My bank account would have ballooned, but I would just be another cog in the machine. It would be hard to stand out. My ambition, however, was bigger than my appetite for money.

Unlike the Japan offer—the organization was already first in the country—going to Beijing involved joining the fifteenth-ranked company with $100 million average annual revenue and propelling it upward.

It was a huge risk because I could have sunk my career, especially with the daredevil strategy I employed, which I will outline in Chapter Four. But I was young and understood that the only way I could continue making a name for myself was by generating a big splash.

TLDR: It was a career move that could have backfired. But I knew that if I wanted to make a difference, I had to think of something bold. Sometimes, you have to leave the haven of safety and head in a direction others wouldn't even imagine.

* * *

I will never forget my roots. Occasionally, I'll read news about senior executives in big companies receiving big, fat bonuses for a job well done and wonder if they, at least, thank their subordinates. Personally, I know that I would never have been where I am without my employees, which is why I always request for more incentives for them when I can. I've never asked more for myself. It was my way of motivating them to work harder for me the next year so that we could get higher incentives. This is rare among top leaders, many of whom would rarely go through the trouble to ask for more for others lest they stir the hornets' nest.

Large multinational companies usually have annual promotion and increment cycles at certain times of the year. Often, managers would either justify not giving a pay raise or promotion, citing uncertain economic conditions or poor overall company performance. I always went in the opposite direction and would give salary bumps and promotions to those who deserve it even before the appraisal period. It never failed. Employees became more motivated and driven, and our company's performance always improved exponentially the following year.

Twenty years ago, when I was the managing director for Korea in Bristol-Myers Squibb, my boss gave me a $100,000 promotional marketing budget for the year and a similar amount of stock options for me. The aim: increase revenue by $1 million. Instead of fussing over media plans and complicated campaigns, I distributed both the budget and stock options to the team, dangling them as incentives. They were already very stretched, so I wanted to motivate them. Naturally, we went above and beyond. The team remained committed and engaged because they didn't expect this bonus.

It's not just about financial compensation. In another episode, also when I was Korea's managing director for Bristol-Myers Squibb, I instituted longer maternity leave. This was during a time when new mothers in the country only had two weeks off after giving birth. I was driving to the office and heard on the radio that Korea was behind the world in this issue, and the government was slowly mandating for companies to push it up to two months of maternity leave to match the rest of the world.

When I reached the office, instead of waiting for the government, I immediately told the HR department to increase maternity leave from two weeks to two months. We were the first company to do it and were featured in the media.

I pushed for something similar at Medtronic. In the past, non-Singaporeans working for the company only received three months of maternity leave, while locals enjoyed an extra month. I was initially unaware of this until one of my employees brought this disparity up. The policy didn't make much sense to me, either, so I suggested that the HR department rectify this discriminatory approach and provide four months of maternity leave to all new mothers in the company.

TLDR: While these are just small anecdotes, it shows how effective small, but surprising, decisions can be to ensure positive outcomes. Furthermore, when these rewards are unexpected, the effectiveness multiplies. The key is to communicate the reason behind your actions to your staff.

History Will Remember Your Actions, Not Your Words

The 1997 Asian Financial Crisis affected Korea badly. The Korean won depreciated immensely. This resulted in scores of foreign investors reducing their exposure in the country and caused multiple bank runs. The International Monetary Fund had to step in to prevent a sovereign debt crisis.

I was working as the country's managing director in a global pharmaceutical company, Bristol Myers-Squibb. Our global headquarters tasked me to restructure the firm and reduce salaries by a whopping 40 per cent. That would have crippled our employees' financial health. Instead of immediately refusing, I asked if the vice president—the person giving the order—would also agree to a similar pay cut to share the pain. Most would have balked at asking such a provocative question to their superior, especially since it could be detrimental to their career progression. But I was focused on the livelihood of my staff. To me, that's what being a maverick meant—testing a path no one had dared to venture into. It would have been easier to nod my head and execute the order, but leadership is demonstrated in moments like this. I was nervous, naturally, but overcame it by telling myself, 'What's the worst that can happen? That he would say no?'

My request perplexed him, and I knew what his answer would be.

After some time, he said he couldn't because it would set a bad precedent for the company. 'Look at that,' I said. 'Don't you hate it too? A restructure that only results in employees suffering is unacceptable.' The vice president had no reply and eventually backtracked on the demand. I used that opportunity to ask for something crazy instead: I pushed for a 10 per cent increase. My reasoning was simple. Because of the won's currency depreciation against the US dollar, the raise I asked for would have barely dented operating profits.

My boss agreed after some convincing. Ultimately, it made financial sense. The productivity and morale gains far outweighed the expenditure. When we announced the move, it made national headlines the next day. Employees' morale skyrocketed. They knew that their leader wasn't just full of empty words, but backed them up with decisive action. Immediately after, some of the top talents in the country wanted to join us. The move solidified the company's reputation as one that values employees. We had no problems hiring from then on. The Korean division would also post record performances in 1998 and beyond.

TLDR: The typical business mindset would have been to cut costs. That's what many companies in Korea did. I went the opposite direction and that resulted in better long-term performance. There is opportunity in a crisis. You only need to stay calm and find it, like I did.

The recent pandemic affected some countries more than others. At one time, an Asian country had the highest number of cases in the world. It also suffered the most. In such conditions, it was impossible for the country team to hit their quarterly sales targets through no fault of their own.

During the town hall meeting in this country, I requested to be the last person to present. I also asked my team not to prepare any slides. After the other senior leaders had completed their speeches—all designed to boost morale—I went up on stage and told everyone in the room that they could forgo their target for the year. Instead, I would give out performance bonuses to everyone, on the basis that they did hit the sales objectives. In moments of suffering like this, encouraging words mean nothing to people. They need something tangible. I thought it was the least I could do to help those struggling.

My decision, and not the speeches, boosted morale and also showed the employees that the company valued them very much. It also didn't cost us a lot, but generated an incredible amount of goodwill. I knew that it would also motivate them to continue working hard for the organization.

TLDR: There's a saying: people don't remember what you said, but they'll remember how you made them feel. It not only applies in your personal lives, but your working relationships, too. Think about who has made the most impact in your own circle. You only remember their decision or action because it made you feel a certain way.

Don't Accept the Status Quo. Instead, Ask 'Why?'

During the early to mid-90s, I was managing the East Asian business operations for MSD, another global pharmaceutical company. Late-night entertainment was a common practice. Sales representatives would treat clients to enormous meals and expensive bottles of wine at business dinners. Because of this, all the sales reps in the industry were male. This was because these meals would stretch on late into the night. Occasionally, the group would also shift to places that had unsavoury entertainment options. While frowned upon now, in the past, this was normal.

I remember asking the head of human resources, 'Why don't we hire female sales reps?' The reply was that it wouldn't work due to the factors mentioned. I was unconvinced. I believed women would bring a different perspective to the table and pressed my case.

My company became the first in the pharmaceutical industry to bring in female sales reps, and my hunch was correct. Imagine having 100 salespeople coming to your office—99 were male and only one was a woman. She would naturally stand out and the client would remember her.

Business metrics across the board improved. The female reps spent longer times pitching with the clients and were not required to stay up late to entertain them. Instead, business was conducted during lunches and casual coffee meetings, and employees came to work visibly more refreshed the next day. I also realized they had more discipline and organization compared to their male counterparts.

The knock-on effects were tremendous. Other companies in the pharmaceutical space began hiring female sales reps after noticing the business benefits. Eventually, gender equity improved.

TLDR: Even in today's business environment, some companies might unintentionally discriminate against a certain group because of perceived ideas, even if they are well-intentioned. Always think if there is a better way to achieve your goals and spot your blind spots. Everyone has them. If you can't find them, ask your trusted peers or mentors; they might see something that you've always missed. Then, remove these blind spots if you can. In time, this action will catalyse your personal, career, and business growth.

The business casual dress code for the office is common now, but this wasn't the case in the 90s and early 00s. Office wear was usually stiff and regimented. I remember seeing Bill Gates paying a visit to Korea when I was at Bristol-Myers Squibb and noted his extremely laid back dress code—mostly sweaters and denim jeans—when visiting some of the most notable political and business leaders.

Back then, and even now, the country still hewed close to traditional forms of dress—a shirt and tie at the very minimum in the office. So, seeing Bill Gates in casualwear made me think: as the leader, if I was the most casually dressed person in the office, then that would encourage everyone else to dress similarly. So, I came up with a 'strict' guideline—you could wear anything you like to the office as long as you don't offend others or have external meetings with clients that day. The HR department added an addendum to the policy: no denim jeans with holes.

I was slightly miffed. The rule was pedantic, overly restrictive, and did not benefit morale, productivity or the bottom-line. It was simply because someone in the department didn't like that item of clothing. The next day, I came to the office in shorts and a T-shirt! That policy was rescinded immediately.

Many in the office appreciated the new policy. Shirts and ties every day can be stifling at best and downright unhygienic, especially during the heat of summer. Of course, those who still wanted to wear their suits were welcome to. The important thing was that the staff had the flexibility to decide how comfortable they wanted to be. And when employees feel empowered, they generally perform better.

In another episode, I dyed my hair to create a more relaxed and creative environment. There was no occasion. I wanted to encourage staff to think out of the box and everything could be questioned. Innovation can only occur when people remove self-imposed constraints and limitations. There was just one problem. At that time, I was severely overweight; I felt really uncomfortable with my body, but hadn't done anything about it. A pudgy man with outrageously coloured hair isn't an image becoming of a CEO. So, I decided it was time to lose weight. In six months, I lost 20 kg. My weight was now a trim 75 kg. I looked younger and my casual attire and dyed hair didn't seem out of place now.

Several of my staff were inspired by my transformation and went on their own respective self-improvement journeys. Many also lost weight, and some picked up new hobbies such as scuba diving and tennis. A few even revamped their wardrobes to follow the old adage, 'Dress for the job you want, not the job you have.'

People were happier and the office seemed more vibrant. While I'm unsure if there were productivity gains, I'm sure many looked forward to coming to work.

TLDR: Empowering others always leads to better outcomes, and it could be just as simple as tweaking a long-standing and seemingly insignificant policy. As a leader, view everything with a questioning glance and always ask if anything in the company can be made better with a small adjustment, such as dying your hair.

Lead from the Front, Not from the Ivory Tower

In large multinational corporations, it's extremely common for employees to never see their CEOs and senior executives beyond scheduled mass town halls or on television screens around the offices. It's normal for staff to find out news about their senior executives from outside sources instead of from within. I find that a shame. It's one reason why innovation and creativity are so difficult in such firms.

And when they do meet the CEO in person, they are quiet and probably even afraid. I should know, I was once a young twenty-five-year-old employee who rode an elevator with my global CEO at that time and didn't say a word because one, I found him familiar but couldn't recognize him and two, I thought it would be rude to ask. The CEO is mythologized to be an all-knowing, all-seeing entity, when the reality is that he or she is probably just as human as any of us and would enjoy genuine interaction.

Today, the CEO who interacts with customers, replies personally to emails and frequently meets with employees is more valued. When you study personalities such as the gregarious owner of the Dallas Mavericks and serial entrepreneur, Mark Cuban, or the charismatic founder of the Virgin Group, Richard Branson, you feel a sense of warmth towards them and feel like you know them even though you've never met them. This ultimately helps with the growth of not only their companies, but their personal brand.

I adopted this approach a long time ago.

For me, the best opportunity to get to know an employee is during the interview. Many leave it to their respective department heads to conduct it. I think it's a missed opportunity.

Being there with the potential hire gives you the chance to demonstrate that you value their time and impress upon them the vision and values of the company. You can also probe their thoughts about the firm—what they feel it's doing well, what can be improved, and so on.

It also gives the employee the chance to ask you, the leader, any questions they desire. There are always lessons to be gleaned from conversations like these.

Most usually ask me for the vision I have for the company. I'm ecstatic to share it with them because I want them to get excited for their future with the organization. I also want to motivate them by sharing that their hard work will be recognized and rewarded. When you get everyone's buy-in, it makes it easier to steer the ship.

After the interview, I also take some time to craft a brief thank-you email to the potential hire. It only takes five minutes of your day, but will probably mean the world to the recipient. Even if they don't join the company, they might spread stories of their positive interaction to friends and peers. Such behaviour takes on even more importance in today's social media world. I'm sure you've read favourable and negative anecdotes about specific leaders and companies written by anonymous posters. By being a force of good to everyone you meet, you can create an outstanding impression of your company through kind leadership.

During onboarding sessions—when new employees are brought up to speed on company processes, culture and more—I also always drop by to say hello. Large companies can feel cold and sterile. So it's important to make your staff feel warmly welcomed. After all, they are the ones turning your vision into reality.

TLDR: Turn bureaucracy into an ally, not your enemy. Bridge the distance between yourself and the people working for you by taking the initiative to say hello to them whenever you can. Large organizations tend to have many layers between the leaders setting the vision and the people actually doing the work. Cut through the fat by simply coming down from the top of your tower to the ground and getting to know the employees personally.

* * *

This might surprise you, but I rarely, if ever, set deadlines for my staff. You'll never hear me say:

- 'Robert, finish the report by this weekend.'
- 'Park, no matter what happens, the project must be completed by the end of the month.'

I strongly believe that using such regimented language and setting strict deadlines leave no room for creativity and innovation. Instead, all you get are machines churning work. We already have ChatGPT by OpenAI and soon, Bard by Google, accomplishing that role.

I want my employees to be invested in their work and proud of the output. So, I usually ask them how long it'll take them to complete the project and the resources they need to ensure that they meet the timeline they've set for themselves. This method has hardly backfired for me. When people are empowered to accomplish a task in a manner of their choosing, they usually will surprise you—in a good way.

When you trust and respect your employees, magical things happen. Reports that are due on Friday will arrive on your desk a few days earlier. More care has been devoted to the facts and figures. I've seen it happen so often in my decades-long management career.

Of course, there are bad apples. They will hand in shoddy assignments or give terrible excuses when missing deadlines. As a leader, it's then your job to shape them up or ship them out. But, I never add unneeded pressure. For example, if an employee has promised to submit work by Friday afternoon but nothing has appeared in your inbox on Friday morning, I refrain from demanding it. This will only backfire in the long run. As a leader, investigate the cause for the tardiness and then decide the appropriate course of action—a reprimand, lesser responsibilities, etc.

And if the report comes close to the deadline in a state unfit for submission, never jump to conclusions and scold the employee, especially in front of others. No one likes to be scolded unfairly. We were all once subordinates, too, doing our best for our superiors. It could be possible that life circumstances might have gotten in his or her way. Once again, understand what happened before deciding what to do next.

Being a boss means ordering people around from your place of comfort to achieve your goals. Being a leader means developing your employees to be the best possible version of themselves. I'll let you decide the kind of manager you want to be.

TLDR: Trust your employees to set their own deadlines, as long as they are within reason. There will be hiccups along the way, but when you work to understand why there are roadblocks, your employees' work will eventually improve. Great things happen when you truly believe in your people.

* * *

Questions to Ponder Over

1. What's the craziest thing you've done in your career that paid off? Similarly, what was the wildest gamble you took that failed?
2. When was the last time you stood up for something you believed in, even if it meant going against someone? What did you stand up for?
3. Think about the best leader you've had in your life so far. What were his or her characteristics that you really liked?

Chapter Four

Becoming Memorable, or Setting Yourself up for Leadership

'The mediocre teacher tells. The good teacher explains. The superior teacher demonstrates. The great teacher inspires.'
—William Arthur Ward, American motivational writer, wrote in the 1960s for his column 'Pertinent Proverbs', which was featured in multiple publications

---

ChrisNotes

- We remember the leaders who achieve crazy things or have outrageous goals, not the ones who play it safe.
- Abraham Lincoln once said, 'Every man can withstand adversity. But if you want to see his true nature, give him power.' Remember this at all times.
- Leaders who remain humble and understand that they don't have the answers to everything go a lot further in life.

I wasn't always a leader. Like many, I started my career from the bottom, selling pharmaceuticals to doctors in America. My father wasn't enthused about my job. He was actually embarrassed. After all, he ran a hospital and managed hundreds of doctors. So, I was determined to make a name for myself in the field and figured that becoming the top salesperson in my then company, MSD, would make him proud.

The only problem was, I didn't know where to start. Every Friday, my office would put up the sales performance chart that ranked everyone's revenue generation on the wall. The top ranking salesperson would always change, but the name propping the bottom remained the same. I was always dead last.

To sell pharmaceuticals, I needed to speak to the doctors and convince them of the products' merits. However, to even smell the sanitized doors of the doctors' offices, I needed to pass the receptionists, who never gave me the time of day. I was stumped.

Then one day, while having lunch by myself, I watched an African-American man try to hawk glasses at the street corner. Nobody was giving him the time of day, too. I empathized with his situation. Soon enough, with only a couple of sales in that hour, he packed up and left. I was about to head back into the office when I saw an older East Asian lady shuffle her way to the same corner, assemble a table and chair, and started selling fortune cookies. She sold more cryptic fortunes in ten minutes than the man sold glasses in an hour. There wasn't anything special about her wares. However, I suspected that her products were appealing because she tapped onto an important truth: that everyone's favourite subject is themselves.

Something clicked in my head. What if I only targeted Asian doctors? I was Asian, after all, and could relate to them better since we had similar backgrounds. Just like the fortune cookie that spoke to the buyer, I could probably understand the doctors' needs better. During that period, in the early 1990s, there were barely any Asian sales representatives like me. I went to Chinatown after lunch and walked into the first clinic I saw.

After introducing myself and giving my name card to the receptionist, I requested to talk to the doctor.

The young lady took one look at the company I was from and immediately rushed into the doctor's office. At that time, MSD was the world's biggest and most successful pharmaceutical company.

I walked out that day from the office not only with a sale, but an exclusive contract with the doctor for a specific medicine. Every day after that, I would pound the pavements of Chinatown, Koreatown, and other East Asian enclaves, and speak to the Asian doctors serving the community. Over time, I captured 90 per cent of the whole Asian market. In four months, I generated US$3.5 million of revenue. To provide some perspective, the average sales generated by an MSD salesperson stood at US$2 million a year. I produced more in four months than everyone in the company did in a year. My name no longer propped up the weekly Friday list. I was the best among 500 or so salespeople in my division.

The following year, in the first quarter, I ranked highest among the 48,000-strong MSD sales force. Until today, my remarkable performance is still remembered by some within the company.

Eventually, I won the Chairman's Award, an annual prize given to the most successful sales representative of the year. The company also started dedicating more Asian sales representatives to cater to the underserved Asian market of doctors.

There is an Asian saying: 'It's better to be the head of a snake than the tail of a dragon.' My experience in MSD taught me that if the door is closed, instead of knocking incessantly on it, try the window. Everyone has a unique strength. Capitalise on it to be successful. I was the only Asian sales representative in the office at that time. I could have wallowed in self-pity, but instead turned it into an advantage and became known as the man with Midas touch in the Asian community. As I climbed up the corporate ranks, I always took this lesson with me: find your niche.

Then, when you do, you must press the advantage.

Take That Crazy Risk

In 1991, during the Gulf War, my company faced a problem. It had penned a contract with a foreign country's government for $6 million worth of vaccines a couple of years ago. Unfortunately, that country—Iraq—was now embroiled in the throes of war.

The Iraqi officials told my company that they could pay in cold, hard cash. The only issue: someone had to fly into Baghdad to pick up the money. Wire transfers were impossible and sending a cheque by air was too much trouble. My company was prepared to write the millions of dollars off as bad debt, but I put up my hand and volunteered to head into the city.

While $6 million might not seem much in the grand scheme, I wanted to show my staff and bosses that I was willing to go the extra mile, even if that mile was in a war zone. Many called me crazy, but I had analysed the situation and believed that the risks were not as precipitous as others thought. The Gulf War was coming to an end and most of the fighting was occurring hundreds of kilometres away from Baghdad.

After I landed, I remember riding in a car trundling along a deserted highway in the city. It was eerily calm with barely any traffic or people. Once I commandeered the money, I returned to the airport to return home. The cash never left my sight.

My bravery and that episode propelled my name into the spotlight among the senior executives in the company. Many of them took notice of me and several remembered me as the man who went into the heart of battle. Even after the war ended and I had left the company, my courageous, some would say foolhardy, actions still popped up in watercooler conversations and boardroom meetings.

Opportunities like these don't pop up often, so when they do, grab them with both hands. You'll be amazed at the mileage you can get with a simple, yet memorable, act.

Remember, at one point in every game-changer's life, many would think them insane. Think of Steve Jobs and Apple, or even Akio Morita and his impossible dream of turning Sony into one of the biggest consumer electronics giants in the world from a humble radio repair shop. Several doubted their dreams, visions and tenacity. But, they persevered. After all, only crazy people change the world.

Treat Everyone with Respect and Appreciate Them

You don't have to go to war or show gory emergency room pictures to your bosses to be memorable. Staying in people's minds can be as simple as going slightly above and beyond their station. I learned this from my father. He was a quiet man, but he let his actions do the talking.

I remember one incident vividly. Three years into his hospital's operations, a boiler on the rooftop exploded and the security guard who happened to be there suffered fatal injuries. He was the sole breadwinner. On the night of the incident, my father woke up and rushed down to be on top of the situation, then spent the next several months looking after the security guard's family without telling anyone. Unfortunately, the guard who passed away didn't have proper insurance.

Almost a decade later, my father introduced a young lady in her twenties to me. I had never met her before, but my father seemed to know her very well. I discovered that this lady was one of the late security guard's children. She was only six years old when her father passed away and my father paid for her education all the way until university. I was flabbergasted.

My father was a quiet man, but his generosity was boundless. During his funeral in 2011, tens of thousands of people came to pay their respects. As one of his five sons, I had to be there on all three days to greet the guests. My brothers and I couldn't recognize 90 per cent of them. We later found out that they were his employees, former patients, the soldiers under his command when he was in the military, and more. We had to extend the funeral from three to five days to accommodate everyone who came.

In Korea and several other East Asian countries, those who come to pay their respects also usually give a condolence envelope containing money (jo-uigeum) to the deceased's family. At the end of the funeral, when we reconciled all the donations, it amounted to millions of dollars. All given voluntarily by people whose lives my late father touched.

While I haven't yet had the opportunity to do such generous deeds, my father's action influenced me greatly. In Korean culture, there are particular honorifics used when greeting people. The more senior ranked you are, the more noble the honorific. This is typical behaviour.

I prefer doing the opposite and reserve the highest honorifics for those who are supposedly below me, such as the cleaners or receptionists. These are the people who can let you perform to your highest potential; so it's vital that you treat them well.

During my last few months in Medtronic, I was travelling to different countries for my farewells. In Korea, there were three senior cleaning ladies who always kept the place spick and span beyond a fault, but I realized that they never received any recognition. Many treated them like part of the furniture. I even saw several closing lift doors in their faces. On my final day, I bought three beautifully wrapped gift boxes filled with beauty products—anti-ageing, moisturising, etc.—for them. They had left for the day, so I gave it to one of my employees to pass to them the day after.

A couple of days later, the same employee sent a photo of the three of them posing with their gift boxes with the biggest smiles on their faces. They also wrote a beautiful thank you note for me, which meant a lot to me because they couldn't write and had to ask someone to transcribe for them.

Everyone deserves respect. To become a leader, you need to learn to manage people's emotions. How do you do that? You empower them and give them the dignity they deserve, no matter where they are in the food chain.

* * *

In the first few months of VentureBlick's inception, a German messaged me unexpectedly. We first met at Bayer. He interned in the Asian office more than a decade ago for about a year. While I remembered his quick wits and smart demeanour, I didn't realize that I influenced his mindset and world view.

When he contacted me, he had rapidly risen through the ranks, becoming a senior executive in the same company. But, over two decades of working in one healthcare company in Europe had made him jaded. He craved a new challenge. He had also followed my progress and thought that it would be the perfect time to reach out again and offer his expertise. He shared with me that he was always impressed by my leadership and always modelled his style after me. For over a decade, he worked under people who didn't garner the same respect and he missed working with someone like me. Incredibly, he even offered to work for free for the first six months so that I could evaluate his competency.

I have similar stories across the globe. In Australia, I offered the country manager role to another man whom I worked with closely a decade ago, but had not contacted since. He told me that he was just about to accept another offer with another company and my overture came at the right time. He always remembered our time working together with fondness and was happy to run it back again, this time with another company. He even told me that he would accept whatever I could afford. 'If we ever become successful, I know that you'll share the wealth with us. That's who you are as a person,' he said.

In Korea, I approached another lady for another role. She was in her 50s and was ready to retire, but I convinced her to push her plans back to help grow the company. She liked the vision I had for VentureBlick and had heard good stories about me from our mutual friends and contacts. And just like the Australian, she didn't ask for much—just enough to ensure that she was eligible for social benefits in the country.

These examples made me jubilant for several reasons. One, it made me feel that my professional career didn't go to waste. Two, it solidified my conviction that doing the right, and the moral, thing always pays off in the long run. Finally, it cemented my belief about what constitutes good leadership.

Ultimately, leadership is working behind the scenes and ensuring that your employees become the best versions of themselves. Allow them to make mistakes and cover for them, and go above and beyond when they ask for support.

You'll see a significant difference in the performances of your charges, which will also ultimately benefit you.

Over-Promise and Deliver

A common corporate maxim always advises you to, 'Under-promise, but over-deliver.' While the psychology behind that saying is sound, I prefer the other path: over-promise and still deliver. The reason is simple—your manager will remember you and your wild promise, and when you do deliver, you'll be known as the employee who can achieve significant targets. On the flip-side, if you fail, a good supervisor will still note your audacity, which is a good thing in the long run.

Of course, I'm not telling you to conjure an impossible aim. Instead, consider your capabilities and the resources you have, and push them to the limits.

For example, in my late twenties, my boss tasked me to look at our company's Taiwanese distribution channels and suggest optimizations. In the report, not only did I give my recommendations, I also proposed cutting our distributor and establishing a presence of our own in Taiwan. The kicker: in the last three pages of the report, I threw my hat in the ring and wrote a detailed breakdown of why I should be appointed the sales and marketing head for the country. I did give a caveat—I knew I was significantly younger than most people in the role, but believed that I could do a better job.

When interviewed, I suggested a promotion if I achieved the company's objectives, and my voluntary resignation if I failed terribly. Naturally, this gave me extra impetus to succeed. (I succeeded, of course. I fulfilled the aims I outlined in the report using the strategies I said I was going to use.)

* * *

One of the most audacious business moves I made catalysed my mercurial rise up the healthcare corporate ranks. It's still talked about to this day, but it could have easily backfired and scorched my burgeoning career.

To this day, I credit this masterstroke for cementing my name in the field.

I had taken over the Chinese division of Bayer, which ranked fifteenth in the country at that time. While the company was expanding, they weren't making much headway in the most populous country in the world. This was before companies were falling over themselves to court the Chinese market, so Bayer was only hiring about 100 people annually, an insignificant number. I studied the market for three months before coming up with a plan-rapid expansion. I wanted to recruit 3,000 people immediately.

The senior management were unbowed. Many didn't think China needed that many people, considering the revenue the market was bringing in. I travelled to the German headquarters eleven times in six months to convince them of my strategy. Once, I even overlapped the country maps of China and Germany to explain why a market of the former's size needed a lot more employees than currently available.

Still, my request was daunting until I pulled out my trump card. If we didn't become the top healthcare company in China within a year, I would leave. Yes, a similar strategy, but a powerful and effective one when deployed effectively. The board relented and I got what I wanted.

Eight months later, we became number one in China, posting over a billion dollars in revenue. The company even overtook healthcare juggernaut Pfizer briefly in the rankings. After my success, the other pharmaceutical MNCs in the country copied my strategy of rapid expansion into second-tier cities. Bayer slowly slid down the ladder again, losing to other firms with deeper pockets, but the effects went long into the future. The brand was seen as reliable and strong, and they became well-known in China, entrenching themselves for years to come.

In the corporate landscape, it's important to stand out if you want to receive leadership opportunities and roles. No one can do a better job promoting yourself than you. In Asian cultures, we tend to downplay our strengths because it's viewed as boasting. While I'm not advocating for you to continuously toot your own trumpet, you should take any opportunity you can to prove yourself to senior management that you are capable of bigger things.

Don't Wear Your Heart on Your Sleeve

It might sound ironic, but displaying a neutral expression at all times is a great tool if and when you become a leader. A manager who oscillates across the emotional spectrum can unsettle staff. You'll become memorable for the wrong reasons.

Several people have asked me why I always maintained a poker face, even in pictures. It's a habit I picked up from my father, who rarely smiled while at work. It wasn't that he was displeased. He believed that showing emotions publicly, whether exuberant happiness or crushing anger, will deaden their impact. If a serious issue or rare event occurs that requires your immediate attention, displaying your rarely-seen emotions will then drive home the importance of that episode. It might spur your staff to also concentrate on solving that problem.

On the flip side, remaining neutral also helps to gain the upper hand at the negotiating table. While I always believe in a win-win relationship, the party on the other side might not feel the same way. If they cannot discern how you feel about particular points in the discussion, they might make beneficial concessions for you.

Once, during a meeting, one of my employees came in at a serious time. He carried a note and passed it to me before exiting as swiftly as he came. I remember unfolding it. The message said, 'Your grandmother has just passed away.' I felt a deep blow to my heart. I was extremely close to her; she raised me when I was young and I owe her so much.

Outwardly though, I maintained a neutral expression. I didn't want to interrupt the discussion. No one realized what had happened. I stayed throughout and only left after the meeting had ended, explaining to my staff that I'll be working from home the rest of the day. None asked if everything was all right; I assumed that they thought I was just feeling slightly under the weather.

I came to the office for the next few days, excusing myself from work a few hours earlier than everyone else to tend to my family affairs. My employees only realized that my grandmother had passed away when the human resources team sent out an official memo. Many came forward to pay their condolences. I accepted them. Several shared with me that they couldn't detect anything wrong based on my facial expression, but felt the slightest change in my behaviour.

* * *

The Western world typically—and stereotypically—embraces outward displays of emotion. You can see it in their social interactions, television shows and films, even serious press conferences. Apple's annual events, when the Cupertino-based firm unveils its latest products, come to mind. Presenters' voices have unusually wide inflections to depict excitement and the language used is more upbeat and enthusiastic.

Asians in the business world, however, are usually more stoic. Beyond staying neutral, we're also more careful with dispensing praise and criticism. Westerners have no such qualms. Compliments are given freely and negative feedback is dished out rapidly, with no concern for the recipient's well-being.

While I'm not against criticism, I believe that there's a time and place to give it. My mantra: when needed or deserved, praise in public and criticize in private.

Compliments are a great motivational tool in the office. However, it loses its effectiveness if used too often. The recipient might even think that you're being disingenuous. A simple rule of thumb is that the effect of the second compliment is usually half of the first. On the flipside, if the praise given is attentive, thoughtful, and unlike any the person has received, my experience is that the positive effects are tripled or even more. It's one reason I go big when praising someone.

During my tenure leading Bristol-Myers Squibb Australia, the top salesperson in each region usually gets a token of appreciation from the company for his or her hard work. In Sydney, one sales executive had topped the pile for three years in a row. I wanted to express my appreciation to him and asked the team in Sydney if any of my predecessors had visited them before. They said no. So, I decided to go by from the head office in Melbourne to Sydney and personally hand the gift to the salesperson. I didn't tell this to them in advance though, wanting it to be a surprise.

The branch office was initially shocked. The manager even thought that the salesperson had made a grave mistake. I kept reassuring them that it was just a routine visit and told them not to make any special preparations. The salesperson offered to pick me up from the airport, but I rejected it gently. I wanted the team to work like it was a typical weekday and didn't need any special treatment. My purpose was to observe the salesperson and understand what set him apart from the rest, so that I, too, could learn and pass on his knowledge and skills to others.

The day went by without a hitch. The following day, I explained the purpose of my visit to the team and shared how impressed I was with the patience, determination and skills of Sydney's top salesperson. At the end of my short presentation, I presented him with a Montblanc fountain pen, which had picked out myself and had his name engraved, a reward for his hard work. I had bought the pen using my own money.

It might have just been a series of small compliments and a smaller gift, but it made a massive impact on the team and the person receiving the pen. I also knew talent such as him would eventually be scouted and poached by bigger companies, and I wanted to express how much the company appreciated him and his efforts.

The salesperson did stay and continue striving. He would remain at the top for years to come. More importantly, the Sydney branch office's revenue also increased, buoyed by my visit.

Don't wear your heart on your sleeve. But, when you do roll them up to reveal it, make sure that you give as much of yourself as you can. You'll definitely become a memorable leader.

Learn Your Weaknesses and Capitalise on Your Strengths

Some of the best lessons I've learned about sales and business actually came from my odd jobs when I was a student. Since I had to support myself when I was studying in the US, I had to take numerous jobs. I've sold cars, scooped ice cream into cups and cones and even drove a taxi. I learned a lot about the fundamentals of selling through these roles.

In fact, one of my most memorable odd job stints was driving the yellow cab in New York City during my university days. Yes, it's those ubiquitous taxis you always see being hailed in films and television shows by the main characters shouting, 'Taxi!' I only worked part-time on the weekends because I had to go to school on weekdays and complete my coursework on some weekends. Yet, I was able to earn over US$10,000 a month on average. That was a significant amount of money in the 1980s. That experience taught me several things about business that I still apply till this day:

1. Find your target customer segment

I was a full-time student then, so I had to make the most money in the shortest time possible. Instead of driving around the city and waiting for customers to hop on, I decided to go to the source of customers. During this period, the Japanese economy was at its peak. Many Japanese tourists, flush with riches, travelled to the US. Noticing this trend, I focused on Japanese customers arriving at the John F. Kennedy International Airport. I was Asian, so the Japanese also preferred taking my taxi. They also usually went to a few particular places in New York not known by normal taxi drivers. This was a time before Google Maps and the Internet wasn't widely available. They were also incredibly generous with their tips!

2. Differentiate your services

Noticing that most Japanese visitors don't speak English well, I prepared vital information in hand-written Japanese, such as a simple area map, and a list of Japanese restaurants or clinics nearby based on the hotel they stayed in. I was familiar with simple Japanese, so it was easy for me to create these. I also accepted both USD and Japanese Yen as payment, which was very rare during that time. I even gave out change in Japanese Yen. At the end of every ride, I also bowed to my customers, which often made them pleasantly surprised since they didn't expect that kind of gesture in a foreign country.

3. Turn one-time customers into repeating clients

Most of the Japanese visitors stayed in New York for at least a week. Since they had travelled so far, they wanted to spend as much time as possible soaking in the sights and sounds. I would give them my phone number and tell them to call me if they ever needed a taxi driver. In the first day or two, they would usually hail cabs like any other New Yorker. However, they soon realized that my service was better than the other drivers. So, they would call me whenever they needed a taxi during their stay in the city. They also referred me to their friends and families. Over time, my phone kept ringing off the hook from referrals and repeat customers. For this reason, I never cheated or tried to overcharge any of my customers, even if they were first-time visitors. I knew very clearly that my dishonesty would spread and I would lose my steady stream of clients. I preferred long-term customer relationships over short-term interests because I know it's more profitable in the long run.

I've applied these three tenets in all my leadership roles. Three decades later, they are still as relevant as ever and have helped me in my never-ending quest to be a memorable and effective leader.

* * *

Questions to Ponder Over

1. It might sound like a cliché interview question, but what is your biggest weakness, and your proudest strength?
2. Tell me about a time you made a promise, whether to yourself or someone else, that you kept. Why did you keep it?
3. What do you want to be remembered for?

Chapter Five

The Differences Between Asian and Western Leadership (And Why the World Needs Asian Leadership Now)

'A leader is best when people barely know he exists; when his work is done and his aim fulfilled, they will say: we did it ourselves.'

—Lao Tzu, Chinese Taoist philosopher from the fifth century BC

ChrisNotes

- The global economy is favouring the Eastern-centric countries, and their cultures are vastly different from those in the West.
- Collaboration and cooperation go further than competition and strife. Collectivist societies are geared towards this.
- The leader of the future needs to be well versed in business practices across the globe.

I have a contrarian view on leadership. While there are no definite answers, a 2017 research paper derived from a debate between two Academic Leadership Fellows Program groups estimated that the genetic component for leadership stands between 24 and 30 per cent.[2] This study has not been peer reviewed and a proper scientific study to delve into this paper has never been commissioned, so we cannot say with any certainty whether leadership is the result of genetic or environmental factors.

Personally, I believe great leaders are born with the potential, but it takes time, experience, self-awareness, and grit to mould that promise into possibility. Another contrarian opinion: leadership isn't just about having the loudest voice in the room or bossing your people around to do your bidding. It's about managing people's emotions, respecting and empowering them, and giving them the dignity they deserve.

I've learnt many lessons from both good and bad leaders. Many of us will experience both in our careers. The key is to pick the good traits from leaders you admire and incorporate them into your own leadership style, and understand the characteristics of leaders that you don't like, so that you can avoid becoming one.

The Western model of leadership generally promotes individual achievements and elevates one man or woman above the rest. I'm sure you've heard of the tired, overused tropes:

- It's a dog-eat-dog world.
- Only the strong survive.
- Move fast and break things.

---

[2] 'Point/Counterpoint: Are Outstanding Leaders Born or Made?' Copyright © 2017 American Association of Colleges of Pharmacy. Available in the National Library of Medicine database.

The problem with these clichés is that they treat people and the environment as disposable, infinite resources. As we teeter from one crisis to another, I propose that it's time for the world to adopt another form of leadership—consensus-based, collectivist leadership, or the Asian way.

* * *

Leadership Lesson One: Demonstrate That You Care for Your Superiors and Staff

I was the first and only Asian to reach the executive leadership level in Bayer's 150-year history. In my first month, I attended an all-hands executive meeting and at the start of it, the then CEO of the company said, 'Chris Lee is the first true commitment that we are hiring an Asian person at this level in the company. We are going for diversity, so we should not speak German during this meeting.'

True to his word, the entire session was conducted in English. The only problem: this meeting was being held during the Lunar New Year period, which is usually an important holiday for East Asian cultures like mine. No one would ever think of holding a meeting during the week of Christmas and New Year. That would be absurd. Yet, here I was attending a meeting during Lunar New Year, which is a more important holiday than Christmas for many Asians.

It taught me an important lesson: your employees are your first customers. I constantly heard the refrain, 'customers first', but I've believed for a long time that this philosophy misses the forest for the trees. If your staff isn't happy to come to work, then how can they be expected to bring joy to their clients' lives? So, I've always focused on lifting the collective happiness of my employees.

This maxim shouldn't just apply to those in customer-facing roles. At various points in an employee's time with an organization, they will interact with vendors, members of the public and more. They essentially are ambassadors or representatives of the company and will negotiate, cajole and reveal secrets, whether you like it or not. Happier employees naturally present a better front for the company and will usually act in its best interests.

One memory I've always taken with me is from an incident a decade ago, when I was first approached to join Medtronic. The then CEO of the organization asked if I could get a former superior to write a reference letter for me, for formality's sake. I approached my previous boss in Bayer and asked him nicely if he could pen one. At the time of my request, he had been living the retired life for about six months, so he had every reason to reject me. Not only did he complete the task, he wrote a ten-page handbook about my strengths and weaknesses and held a two-hour-long phone call with Ishrak. The latter remarked that it was the best reference he had ever received in his corporate life.

It's not the first time that the good doctor did such a generous deed for me. Prior to this book you're reading now, I wrote and published two other books focusing on effective emotional management and great marketing practices. The sales and training department at Bayer purchased a large quantity of the latter for their own purposes without any undue influence from me. In fact, I only knew about it after the sale had been made. Still, at that point in history, there was still Asian hate fomenting in small sections of the company and these bigots thought this was the best time to oust me from the company, so one of them reported me to the compliance department for conflict of interest. An officer was then dispatched to my office to investigate the allegations.

As part of the investigations, I had to testify in front of the disciplinary committee in Germany. My boss was there, standing beside me to give me both moral and physical support. He also demonstrated his immense trust in me by putting his career on the line and telling the members of the jury, 'I know Chris. He can be wild and unsystematic. But he's also the cleanest person I've ever met. If even one Euro is misappropriated because of Chris, I will leave the company.' His faith in me never wavered.

His acts left an indelible impression on me, and I've always strived to do the same for anyone under my management.

One of my unshakeable leadership beliefs: letting your employees make mistakes, within reason, of course. When you allow them to fail, you also give them room to grow and learn. On the desk of former American president Harry Truman, there was a sign that said, 'The buck stops here.' It was Truman's lifelong motto, and one that he regularly applied in his presidential tenure. I identify strongly with that concept and have always taken responsibility for my staffs' mistakes, especially if I believe that those employees have lots of potential. As a senior leader, I also usually have more leeway and thus, forgiveness, with the board.

This approach doesn't just stop in the office. I remember an incident when my best performing sales representative tied the knot. As a wedding present, I passed him the keys to my BMW so that he could drive to the airport for his honeymoon. On his way there, he got into an accident. He could have sunk into deep trouble with the authorities because he wasn't supposed to be driving my car, so I took full responsibility and paid for the damages.

He was incredibly contrite and I forgave him because I knew that he didn't have any malicious intent. He would go on to be a long-serving, loyal employee.

I've also had employees making critical mistakes that led to the company losing contracts with large hospitals and big medical institutions. None of them acted maliciously or made those mistakes on purpose and in many cases, they immediately understand the error of their ways. I've always believed that there's no point in scolding them; they are adults, too. I just have a quiet word with them in private and display my support for them publicly. They rarely, if ever, make the same mistakes again and also always support my decisions.

When you take the time to understand your employees and let your actions show that you care for them, they will go to the ends of the earth for you.

* * *

Decades ago, in my late twenties, I was at the helm of the newly created Korean division of a large multinational pharmaceutical company. I was also responsible for setting up the physical office and had to hire an interior designer, contractors and other specialists. To get the office ready in time for the opening, they had to work weekends and occasionally even work from sundown to sunrise.

I had never seen construction work before, and occasionally visited the site to check on progress and learn how everything was put together. On one of those visits, I saw a middle-level manager amongst the debris. He had gloves on and was caked in dust, but diligently picked up the trash and placed them in the designated bins. I was impressed.

A day before the official opening, I went down one more time. While the major works were completed, there were still several minor details that needed tying up—throwing the trash, setting up the coffee machines, putting the chairs where they needed to be, etc. Without hesitation, I rolled up my sleeves and went to work. The same manager was there, too, and we took a photo together that day. I asked him why he did something that wasn't part of his job scope and his reply floored me. 'It's my company. So, why not? Most younger employees won't do it and they might sue you. That's why I never made a big fuss about doing this. I just hope that the employees might be inspired to follow me.'

He didn't crave attention or validation, just the quiet satisfaction of a job well done. Seeing him inspired me to do as much as I can for my people without expecting anything in return. I'm glad to say that my small actions have also inspired a legion of staff. Today, these gestures—opening doors for people, helping service staff with the pastries, etc.—are a part of my personality and I do them without thinking.

Your employees and superiors will notice this behaviour, especially if you do it consistently over time. Your actions create a deeper and longer-lasting impact than a stirring speech or a grand gesture.

Leadership Lesson Two: Details and Perspectives Matter

The next time you travel to America or Europe, track down a physical world map and study it. You'll notice something interesting, as I did many years ago during my own travels. World maps in the US will always put America in the middle while those in Europe naturally place their region in the middle.

It's one of the reasons China, Japan, Taiwan, Southeast Asia and more are known as the Far East even though it doesn't make sense from a geographical perspective—any part of the world can be the Far East depending on your location. When the British ventured to our part of the world in the 1800s to expand its colonies, they went eastwards. Hence, anything beyond India was known as the Far East, and the term has stuck until today.

I've seen Western managers sign official documents with a red pen when on a business trip to China, Korea, and Japan. While perfectly acceptable in most parts of the world, writing or signing your name with red ink in China, Korea, and Japan is a cultural taboo. It signifies that one's life is at an end and death is near. I've even seen country leaders get upset when they see this.

I've also observed several instances of ignorant leaders joking about the missing fourth floor in many buildings in China, not realizing that the number 4 is considered unlucky because it sounds like the Mandarin word for death.

I bring these small anecdotes up to demonstrate the power of perspective. As a leader, you'll be faced with many tough, hairy situations that occasionally demand almost instantaneous decisions. In many of those times, you will usually look at the state of affairs from your lens—and with your lens, Singapore will always be in the far east.

But, when you shift your map, you'll open up an entirely new perspective. It sounds demanding, but being a great leader demands that you change your worldview and study the details.

* * *

When I led the Asia-Pacific division of Medtronic, one of the hardest markets I handled was Japan. Don't get me wrong, the people working there were fantastic and contributed heavily to the division's growth. However, the Japanese staff always had this perception that they were the largest market in the world after the US, and constantly campaigned to be a separate business entity away from Asia-Pacific.

During town hall meetings in Japan, I regularly shared how the country stacked up against the rest of the countries in Asia-Pacific, but it always fell on deaf ears. Then, I had an idea. In one of the presentations, I shared a bar chart of the different countries' productivity, but I removed identifying marks. Then, I asked the staff to vote and guess which bar belonged to Japan. They were shocked when they found out that Japan actually ranked second to last in the region for productivity. That was the first time they realized how far they had steadily lagged behind and how much room for improvement there was. After that day, the Japanese division no longer asked to be a separate business entity.

This anecdote is not meant to be a damning verdict on Japan. In fact, in my travels, I've realized every country has their blind spot. For example, in Singapore, ask any local on the street where the most delicious food in the world is and they'll likely reply Singapore. Similarly, if you head to Bangkok, India or any other similar thriving metropolis with a buzzing food culture, all of them will probably shout with gusto that their city has the most delectable cuisines.

To be a good leader, it's important to have multiple perspectives and absorb different cultures. One positive, albeit sneaky, trick I use to endear myself to the people of the country I'm in is to always reply that their country's food is 'absolutely delicious' whenever they ask what I think of their local cuisine. It doesn't hurt anyone, isn't a malicious comment, and goes a long way in building good relationships.

* * *

When I was at Medtronic, there was an Indian-American employee who regularly performed well at work. However, his career plateaued at a certain level despite his above-average performance. I wasn't his superior, but he came to me for advice on getting over this hump. I suggested an international exchange and proposed Japan for several reasons. One, while the country had 3,000 staff, it barely had any foreign employees. Second, no one would expect him to go to that country, which is why it would create a larger stir in the company.

Off he went for two years, the only non-Japanese in a team of 200 people. We had multiple conversations during that period and I asked him if he was having a difficult time. He used to only eat Indian dishes. A year into the exchange, he told me, 'When it comes to food, I'm now a very flexible person.'

When he returned, he received a promotion, leaving his career plateau behind. His overseas assignment, which demonstrated his capabilities in a different market, increased his stock in the company and catalysed his rise. Sometimes, all it takes is a change of scenery for someone to push themselves further than ever before. It also helped to be the only Indian person in the team. His work stood out even more.

He's not the only one. I always push for my employees to head overseas, when possible. One of my Korean staff went to the Philippines for several years; now, he manages one of the largest pharmaceutical firms in the world. Several other Asians who followed my advice and went for postings to different countries other than their home market also became successful.

Staying in your birth country might give you a sense of safety and sanctuary, but if I can borrow an oft-used cliché: 'A ship is safe in the harbour, but that's not what ships are built for.' Unfurl your sails.

Leadership Lesson Three: Optimizing Staff's Emotions

The year 1998 was a nadir in Korea's modern history. The Asian Financial Crisis had dented the country's economy severely and the government sought a bailout from the International Monetary Fund (IMF). The two entities came to an agreement, but at severe cost to Korea. The country agreed to a laundry list of economic restrictions, such as:

- Slashing government expenditure
- Liberalisation of trade
- Curtailing Korean conglomerates' expansion overseas
- Tightening monetary policy and more

These actions, while slowly stabilising Korea's economy in the long run, resulted in massive short-term pain. Unemployment stood at close to 7 percent in 1999 and 80 percent of Korean households had lower income due to unemployment, wage cuts and retrenchments. Those were trying times.

During that period, I was leading the Korean division of Bristol-Myers Squibb (BMS). While the company was relatively new in the country, there was a lot of chatter among employees that it might close. In Chapter Three, I shared how I pushed global headquarters to give everyone in BMS a hefty pay raise at that time instead of cutting salaries. It not only demonstrated the company's commitment to the country, but portrayed to others that BMS was a great firm to work in.

To further improve the psychological mindset of staff, I held an event that many would consider bizarre, even downright insane. For five days and four nights, we held an outdoor party at Phoenix Snow Park, a ski resort in the county of Pyeongchang. When everyone was tightening their belts, we were eating, drinking and partying on the company's dime.

This incident went viral. Several industry leaders criticized the party we threw, calling me brash, irresponsible and tone-deaf. Other employees within the same field, I'd imagine, felt envious, at least according to the feedback I received.

Ultimately, those who slammed my actions didn't matter because they didn't influence or contribute to the company's performance. However, my staff worked harder than ever before. They knew their leaders had their backs even in times of crisis, and propelled BMS Korea to the top in the country.

* * *

BMS Korea's bottom-line grew rapidly in the years after the 1998 Asian Financial Crisis. Besides Seoul, the company had four offices in other regions, including Busan, Daegu, Gwangju, and Daejeon. Most of our branches did well, save for the latter, which kept coming in last despite my team's best efforts, such as cajoling the Daejeon manager, who then threatened to quit. It had come to the point that the country's performance would improve if I closed the Daejeon branch.

I thought about the situation and had a plan, but I needed to pay the employees stationed in that county a visit. I instructed my secretary to book the best restaurant in the city and invite staff and their families for a meal.

There was tension in the air on the day of my arrival. Many thought that I had come to announce the closure of the branch and wanted to give them one last good meal before cutting them off, like a prisoner on death row being served their final repast. Like everyone else, I also brought my wife along with me.

The atmosphere in the restaurant was gloomy and pessimistic, with most waiting for the proverbial axe to fall. Towards the end of the meal, I stood up to make my long-anticipated announcement. There was no axe, just apologies. I told everyone present that I took full responsibility for their non-performance, attributing it to poor motivation, an unsavoury office environment, and Seoul's inability to provide appropriate support.

My gamble: giving the Daejeon branch their bonuses as though it had hit the sales target, breathing a new lease of life to their dated office interior with better office equipment and a fresh coat of paint, and finally, providing all sales staff with a car to make it easier for them to do their jobs. I even gave everyone chocolates and cakes to bring home after the meal.

Everyone was shocked. There was also the psychological effect of having their partners at the dinner. They would be intrinsically motivated to perform better for their families.

Three months after this dinner, miraculously, the performance of the Daejeon branch began improving.

Eventually, over several months, it became the top performing county in Korea, beating even Seoul.

My reasoning was simple: if you show people that you genuinely care not only through words but actions, they will feel slightly embarrassed for not performing to your standards. Then, they will get fired up to perform better and live up to your expectations, not only to please you, but also themselves.

* * *

It isn't always hunky dory. There were times in my career when I had to deal with unhappy employees. My approach to them, however, remained the same—treat everyone with dignity and give them the respect they deserve, no matter their station in life.

During my time leading the China division of Bayer, one of my managers in Anhui let go of an employee because of his poor work performance. On any other occasion, this wouldn't be a cause for concern. But the staff in question was incensed by the dismissal, and demanded to speak to me in person because his manager allegedly told him that I had approved of the firing (even though this situation didn't cross my desk).

The man travelled to the head office in Beijing and even slept in the lobby for several days. He refused to leave until I showed up. He had a large bag beside him and my observers reported that it was bulging with unidentified items. Most leaders, I assume, would have paid no heed to this dissenter and probably gotten security, or even the local police force, to remove him from the premises. But I wanted to hear him out. So, I entered the office through the back door to prepare myself first before meeting the man, who was still waiting for me in the lobby.

My staff initially feared for my safety and wanted to put a guard in the same room with the man and me, but I dismissed their concerns. My priority was to hear this man out and if he tried to get violent, I told my staff I would shout for help immediately. I am also trained in taekwondo, so I know how to handle myself.

We had nothing to fear.

The man broke down during our conversation, which lasted for two hours, and said that he needed this job to care for his family and ailing mother. On my end, I shared the struggles of the company at that time and how his manager was also put in a difficult position to trim costs. I also told him that I had reviewed his performance and also found it lacking. I believe in transparency and sharing the truth with anyone who asks. But, being truthful doesn't mean you have to be unkind to people.

I told him that I couldn't give him his job back for several reasons, the topmost being how everyone in the company had seen his behaviour in the lobby for three straight days and would be apprehensive around him if he returned. But I was more than happy to put in a good word and act as his reference if he found a suitable role and needed one.

He appeared remorseful and apologized for his actions. I told him I accepted it. He also agreed to leave the lobby and thanked me for agreeing to meet him. Before we parted ways, I gave him a token sum to help tide him over during this period until he found another job.

Managing people's emotions effectively doesn't always mean giving in to their demands or whims. The key is to listen to understand, not reply, and see the world from their perspective. From there, you can then make more sound, nuanced decisions.

Leadership Lesson Four: Promote Equality Across the Organization

In most democratic countries, equality is enshrined in their constitution. Neither the government nor entities linked to it can deny a person's right to live freely within the legal parameters set by whoever has been voted into power. It's a noble goal, but while the constitution is absolute, humans are varying shades of grey.

Schisms exist within societies. And while all of us try to be impartial, I'm sure the occasional stereotype creeps into our mind when we deal with people. The key is to not let this intruder meddle with how you treat everyone around you.

Similarly, inequalities exist in any organization. The janitor might be treated differently simply because of his or her position; peers from different races are shunned by the rest simply because of the colour of their skin; the CEO is always given the best seat in the house by virtue of his or her standing.

They might be unconscious behaviours, but that does not make it right. As a leader, you must be self-aware enough to detect if inequality has taken root in your team, department and organization, and weed it out.

I am an egalitarian. It's a world-view fermented by my father and shaped after years of being treated as an afterthought in many Western-centric organizations unused to seeing an Asian within their leadership midst. It even happens within Asian countries.

* * *

It was the early nineties. I was the Asia-Pacific regional manager at that time for MSD and based in Hong Kong. Together with four project managers, we made a visit to the headquarters of one of the world's largest electronic conglomerates in Korea to conduct market research. The company was hospitable to a fault, showing the five of us around their massive production lines churning out semiconductors and electronic components. It even scheduled a visit for us to the local art museum.

At the end of the tour, the guide brought us to the reception room. On the table in the room were four sets of souvenirs, filled with a camera and other knick-knacks. The guide then presented my four project managers with them. There was none for me.

The reason was apparent. I was the only Asian in the group. I was also the youngest. The rest were Americans and far older than me. Even though I was their superior, the guide had automatically assumed that I was their assistant because of my ethnicity and age.

I won't lie. At that point, I was hurt. One of my teammates tried to secretly give me the souvenir after realizing that there was none for me, but I quietly shook my head.

On the way back, the Americans discussed the situation. All of them couldn't understand why the gifts weren't equally distributed. I stared out of the window, contemplating the incident. What could I have done to correct the situation? In that moment, I realized that the discrimination wasn't a reflection of my character, but a demonstration of their close-mindedness. So, I strove to never behave similarly and to treat everyone equally, no matter their race, rank or position in life.

Be curious, not judgemental.

I try to spread this ethos wherever I go. Once, I was invited to a farewell ceremony of a senior executive who was leaving the department after being promoted to another role within the global organization. I was invited to say a few words.

'It's great to have a farewell ceremony when employees leave the company. However, in the future, I hope that all employees will be treated the same, and that the person's rank doesn't change the grandeur of the farewell ceremony. The size of the commemorative plaque should be the same, too,' I shared.

'Some employees leave without a plaque and farewell ceremony, even after working for the company for a long time. It is discriminatory to treat one like this simply because they are ranked lower in the company. We should treat everyone the same. This should apply equally to all seniors and juniors.'

It might have seemed abrasive to some, but that small speech galvanized everyone within the company. They knew my approach to leadership and that I would never discriminate knowingly or unknowingly.

From then on, anyone who left—even janitors—always received a small parting gift. I made sure to advocate for equality in every company I had the fortune of helming.

* * *

Questions to Ponder Over

1. Putting aside science and research, do you believe that leadership is a genetic trait? Or can it be nurtured?
2. What do you think are the differences between Asian and Western leadership, if there are any?
3. Share with me some instances in your career that made you feel small because you were misunderstood due to cultural differences.

Childhood & Youth Photos

1965, 100 days old

Taken when I turned 100 days old; I was dressed like a girl because after
having three sons, my mum was hoping I was a girl

1970, Five years old

I'm the youngest boy in the beige coat, probably eating something.
This was taken with my grandparents, uncle, cousins, and brothers
at my father's PhD graduation ceremony at Seoul National University

1973, Eight years old
Taken with my class teacher and classmates, probably
for a classmate's farewell; I am on the far left

1980, Fifteen years old
Stuck in my room, expected to be studying

1980, Fifteen years old

Learning to play the guitar before I took up drums

1981, Sixteen years old

At a ski resort in Korea called Dragon Valley, where the 2018
Winter Olympics were later held

1982, Seventeen years old

Me (right) with a friend during a high school senior year school trip

1982, Seventeen years old

Taken in Osaka, Japan, where I spent a few high school years

1983, Eighteen years old

At my high school graduation in Korea

1984, Eighteen years old

With friends at my high school graduation in Korea (second from left).
A few months later (May 1984), I went to the US

1983, Eighteen years old

Pretending to study for the college entry exam, but thinking about my music; I scored so low for that test and my teacher was surprised

1984, Nineteen years old

At Times Square in New York City. Taken during the Thanksgiving holidays. I had to take a two-hour train from Long Island to NYC just to get a meal because everything was closed

1986, Twenty-one years old
On the lawn of the University of Arizona in Tucson, Arizona, USA

1988, Twenty-three years old
Graduation day from the University of Arizona in Tucson, Arizona, USA

Maverick Moments & Career Highlights

2004

At Taronga Zoo Sydney. I was the Managing Director for ANZ at Bristol-Myers Squibb, I had dyed my hair blonde to show people they can feel free to be different in the office

2017

Costumes are a good way to make your presentations interesting. You can always wear something unexpected to make the audience curious. In this occasion, I was in China Macau, China, for an annual all-employee CSR event (about 1,000 employees)

2017

Riding in on a bicycle as part of the conference opening speech at an employee conference in Macau, China, to about 5,000 attendees

2018

Dressed up as Santa Claus to give out gifts to employees of Medtronic China, ringing in the festive season

2019

Career highlight—putting on the most elaborate outfit I have
ever worn—to entertain employees at an awards ceremony. More than
500 employees were in attendance

2019

Performing as the Phantom of the Opera to surprise and entertain
the top performers at a Medtronic President's Club trip in London

2021

Pretending to be Elvis for a music video to entertain
employees in the middle of the pandemic

2021

Mimicking a rockstar for the Medtronic Asia-Pacific annual
employee kick-off meeting for the theme 'We Rock'

Career Highlights

2012

With the founder of Medtronic, the late Earl Bakken in Hawaii

2018

With Omar Ishrak, the former global CEO of Medtronic, in Australia

2019

Winning the Most Respected CEO of the Year award in Korea

2022

Marking my ten-year Anniversary and Farewell at Medtronic with employees at the Asia-Pacific HQ in Singapore

2022

Celebrating the first day at the Singapore VentureBlick office with cake!

2022

Taken as the Founder & CEO of VentureBlick with the
VentureBlick bear, our little marketing mascot

2022

At our VentureBlick office in Korea, showing off our company hoodie

2023

As a startup founder, I play many roles including helping
the team carry and set up banners for an event

2023

Now as a startup founder I work with a much smaller team than I was used to, but I know every one of them on a much deeper level

2023

Celebrating my first birthday as an entrepreneur at fifty-eight

Chapter Six

Being Human, or How to Make Everyone Perform at Their Best

'You don't manage people; you manage things. You lead people.'
—Grace Brewster Hopper, computer scientist, mathematician, and US Navy Rear Admiral, who said this during a speech she gave at her 1986 retirement ceremony from the Navy.

ChrisNotes

- Artificial intelligence might replace a lot of jobs, but there's nothing to fear if we double down on humanity.
- When you treat people like people and value their contributions, amazing things will happen.
- The scales have tipped far too much in favour of shareholders and profiteers. It's time to tip the balance back.

You must have read the deluge of news and opinion pieces about artificial intelligence (AI) lately. Scrolling through them, it's plainly obvious there are two camps: those who believe that AI will speed up human potential, freeing us from mundane administrative and repetitive tasks, and another group who are convinced that it will become our new overlord. It might surprise you to know that luminaries such as physicist Stephen Hawking and entrepreneur Elon Musk, before he became this polarising figure, sat in the latter group. They wrote cautionary tales and opined that 'AI can end the human race if deployed wantonly'.

I've always believed that you cannot stop technological progress. Change is a given; it's how we react to it that guides our actions. While I, too, am monitoring the development of AI, I don't fear it. Yes, with every major leap, jobs will be lost. But, more opportunities will be created; you only need to grab them.

Several have asked for my thoughts on AI and my philosophy throughout the decades, from the advent of the Internet to Web 3.0 and now the dawn of self-learning algorithms, remains the same: double down on being human.

In business and in life, you'll always interact with people from all walks of life. While the tools always change, the wielders remain the same, and success involves empowering those around you to perform at their best for you.

When I started VentureBlick, one of the first things I considered was employee engagement. Startups usually place staff empowerment at the bottom of their priorities, citing cash-strapped reasons. I thought differently. The vast majority of people who join me on this adventure are taking enormous risks. They could have opted for a larger organization with deeper pockets and some semblance of stability, but they believed in VentureBlick's vision enough to come on board. It was only right that I introduced different means and ways to treat them better, to treat them like a human being.

For example, the company pays for all employee's lunches and snacks. Occasionally, some meals set me back over $1,000, an eye-watering company expense to some. On average, our monthly lunch bill is in the five-digit figure.

A few have asked me, 'Why do you do this? Why have you taken on such a huge financial responsibility even before the company is generating revenue?' My reasoning is simple: when you treat employees like decent human beings, your investment in them will reap manifold rewards in the future. I am sincerely fine with generating lesser revenue in the beginning if it makes my employees happy and proud to be working for VentureBlick.

The many multinational corporations I've worked at have near bottomless resources. Yet, I've sincerely felt that all of them lacked the warmth of humanity. There was a lack of respect for people and the inability to win over people's hearts.

The most opportune time to show your humanistic leadership, no matter the position that you are in, is during periods of change and economic downturns. The upheaval in the tech industry such as Twitter in 2022 and 2023 is a great example. When Elon Musk acquired the social media company in October 2022 for US$44 billion, he went on a firing spree, cutting thousands of jobs citing 'bloat' while promising to 'return free speech' to the digital equivalent of the town square.

At the end of 2022, I interviewed a laid-off employee who shared with me that her firing was sudden and cold. The day after Musk's takeover, her inbox pinged with an email stating that her access to company servers had been severed and that she had to leave the premises immediately.

Similar stories like this can be found everywhere in the digital sphere, of employees getting their access cut and dumped unceremoniously with no proper severance procedures.

Former employees interviewed by *The Washington Post*[3] mentioned that some of the fresh changes Musk, an avid

---

[3] https://www.washingtonpost.com/technology/2023/02/16/elon-musk-twitter/

Twitter user, has rolled out on the site are meant to improve his own experience, including bumping his tweets to the top of his followers' feeds. Musk and his team have also reinstated accounts of incendiary, far-right individuals who promoted violence and hate in the past. Free speech, it seems, will now have no consequences on Twitter.

It has also cost Musk, greatly. Large clients such as Coca-Cola and Nestle either dramatically reduced or stopped advertising their spending on Twitter, with some estimates that revenue dropped by 40 per cent in the weeks leading up to, and the months after Musk's takeover.

Being less than human does have financial repercussions, after all.

The four examples I've outlined over the next several pages drive home the point that doubling down on humanity is your best bet to survive, and thrive, in a world that's hellbent on incorporating AI, no matter the cost.

1: Don't Sweat the Small Stuff

In December 2022, Korean rail workers—train drivers, maintenance employees, frontline staff, etc.—who were part of the Korean Railway Workers' Union planned to go on strike until their wage demands were met. The management refused to accede until a few hours before the planned strike. If the workers had gone through with their threats, the financial damage would have been in the millions because of productivity losses and possible future penalties imposed by the government.

What were the workers' demands? Dropping plans to cut the workforce and agreeing to a paltry 1.4 percent increase in their annual pay. On average, each worker received a monthly increment of 87,000 won (US$143). To put these numbers into context, railway operator Korail had an operating revenue of 4.4 trillion won (US$3.4 billion) in 2020.

While I am wary about using the threats of strikes and public demonstrations to get your way, I was surprised that the argument was just over a 1 percent increase. Unions and employees don't immediately threaten strikes when there are disagreements. There are usually negotiations beforehand and a strike is the last resort, so management must have thought that rejecting the small increment was worth the possible chaos.

If I was Korail's management, I would have gone left, instead of going right (see Chapter Three) and given more than what the workers were asking for. Since it was only a 1 per cent increase, I would give double what they were asking for—a 2 per cent increase—assuming the numbers made sense. At the same time, I would ask for reassurance and have a written agreement that there would be no strikes for several years.

I've had experience dealing with strikes. Previously, when I led the Asia-Pacific division of Bayer, I had to negotiate salaries with the union leader tasked to lead discussions. In Korea, labour unions can be extremely forthright and even militant; there have been cases when union leaders hurt themselves in front of the management team or even attempt to commit suicide by jumping off buildings if their demands are not met.

When the union leader left the room after negotiating with me, he had a smile, which surprised many people who were expecting loud verbal altercations. Unlike the railway workers' demands, which felt reasonable to me, the financial ultimatum from the union leader was too excessive. Instead of cajoling with the man, however, I strived to be as transparent as possible.

I shared with him from the beginning that I knew he was going to ask for a hefty 30 per cent increase, which is financially impossible. And his previous unsavoury experiences with management conditioned him to receiving an initial offer of a 1 per cent increment. I then said I was going to offer him the maximum permissible increment from the start—6 per cent.

We shook hands immediately.

When people feel that they are valued, they will perform better at work. Negotiating downward from a financial request won't make the person believe that the company has their best interests at heart. Giving someone more than what they are expecting, albeit with conditions that make sense, will endear them to you and your company.

At VentureBlick, while we might be a startup, I have an unwritten financial guideline. For those who are earning below a certain amount before joining us, we offer them a decent pay bump. For those with more significant pay packages, we try our best to either match it, give some equity in the company or promise performance-related bonuses.

These are on top of other benefits that include half days on Fridays, the aforementioned lunch expenses and more. These employees are working to make my vision a success and therefore, I believe it's only fair to reward them.

My father rubbed this worldview on me. When he ran his hospital, he created possibly one of the most generous benefit programmes in Korea during the 1980s. They were simple gestures—leasing buses for the employees' work commute, free meals for everyone and their families, and more. Of course, his actions pale in comparison now to the amenities and perks that some of the biggest tech companies in the world provide to their employees. Back then, however, he didn't need to offer that.

I once asked him why. His answer was simple: he wanted to show his appreciation for those who worked for him and these benefits were just minutiae on the bottom-line. His simple actions paid off handsomely for the hospital.

2: Shareholders vs Employees

As a senior executive or professional manager of any listed company, you have a responsibility to make your organization as financially strong as possible. You are there to make money.

There is no debate about that. The question, however, is: how much money do you want to make?

Lately, I believe that the scale has shifted far too much to making money at the expense of the employees who are generating this revenue. The company wouldn't be able to make money without this staff. Having been in the healthcare industry for over three decades, I have seen the insane profits some companies make and the arguments that they peddle to justify these huge green numbers—they contend that high research and development costs eat away at the pie. I don't buy it.

For example, in 2020, Pfizer's CEO Albert Bourla shared with *TIME* that he was expecting the company to make very marginal profits from the Covid-19 vaccine. Yet, a year later, it forecasted $33.5 billion in sales just from vaccines.[4] How? It charges wildly different prices to different countries for its vaccines, and has pushed for annual boosters.

While it's true that Pfizer invested over a billion dollars in R&D before the vaccine received regulatory approval from the FDA, or Food & Drug Administration, it also enjoyed funding—in the billions—from the US government to expand manufacturing capabilities and increase production.

In my opinion, escalating healthcare costs is an epidemic and needs to be fixed, badly. Rich countries can afford the higher prices, but poorer regions are struggling with the higher prices of not just vaccines, but medication. And everything is done in the service of increasing profits at the expense of making the world healthier and better. Wealth should, and must, be better distributed for the world to heal.

The continuous pursuit of profit at all costs has placed the world in a precarious state. Beyond healthcare, the most

---

[4] https://www.nytimes.com/2021/05/04/business/pfizer-covid-vaccine-profits.html

obvious example is climate change. It's time to stop prioritizing shareholders over employees, and approach decisions from a humanistic perspective.

3: The Human Is in the Details

Once, I had to fly to Australia for a series of work meetings and took the company corporate jet. The sun hadn't even peeked behind the cloak of darkness when I landed—it was four in the morning. Yet, a representative from Medtronic was waiting at the airport terminal. I learned she had been there since 10 p.m. the previous day because there was no transport after midnight.

When we arrived at the hotel, I discovered that the company didn't book a room for her. I was flabbergasted and immediately asked the front desk to set aside one for her so that she could rest for the day. I paid for it.

She didn't stay too long; there was work she had to complete, but she expressed her appreciation to me for noticing and caring. She explained she had done these many times before for other visiting senior leaders. However, I was the only one to book a room for her.

Treating employees as humans and not cogs in a machine can even apply to the smaller things. I've regularly seen my leadership peers cancelling meetings on a whim because something urgent cropped up or they felt unwell. While life happens, I'm fully aware that many of the employees stayed up late on many nights to work on these presentations. Rubbing off their appointments from the calendar at the last minute shows how little you value their time, which isn't a good look. If I definitely have to cancel a meeting or presentation because of unforeseen and unavoidable circumstances, I'll ask for the email addresses of all those who are supposed to be present and write them a short note, thanking them for their time and explaining the reasons behind the cancellation.

This separates a good leader from a great one: their ability to notice the insignificant details, especially regarding their staff. There is a saying: employees don't leave a company, they leave their bosses. While financial compensation can keep someone in an organization, vision, belief, and trust in their direct superiors pushes them to achieve more.

I've always put employee satisfaction as a key priority, and I've believed this has helped me in my meteoric rise on the corporate ladder. It doesn't have to be big gestures. Some actions I've practised include:

- Not scheduling meetings on Mondays (as much as I can)
  No one enjoys preparing for a meeting on the first day of the work week, especially with the CEO. It usually means they have to devote some time on the weekend to either prepare presentation slides or gear themselves up mentally. No one likes that, not even me. That's why my first meetings of the week tend to be on Tuesdays.
- Leaving the office on time
  It might seem small, but by leaving the office earlier, I send a message to the rest of my staff that I value work-life balance and want them to head out of the office on time, too. This minor act takes on even more importance in some Asian work cultures, where employees stay beyond their working hours to 'show face' because their boss is still in the office.
- Placing younger or junior employees first in my agenda
  When I have to oversee several presentations, I usually ask my team to put the junior employees at the front. It's not because I want to stress them out. Rather, these events tend to overrun the allotted time period and I'll have to postpone the last two or three presentations. By putting them first, I want to show them that their work is important and I value it.

- Admonish mistakes in private
  I've also seen several senior executives berate their employees, either in public or in front of their peers. I sincerely believe that this isn't beneficial to both parties. The employee doesn't remember the mistake, just the emotional reaction from the dressing down he or she received—'why would my boss scold me in front of other people?!'—while the leader won't receive a productivity boost from the staff. I prefer doing it in private. These actions show a leader's respect for his or her employee.
- Spending as much time as needed in critical moments
  Every manager will eventually have uncomfortable conversations with their employees. It could be something as simple as explaining to an employee the reasons for his or her negative appraisal to as drastic as asking them to leave the company. Most people, including leaders, shun face-to-face meetings when dealing with issues like these. They would rather ask someone else to do the dirty work while they watch from an arm's length or worse, inform the person over a phone call or email. I believe it's important to spend as much time as possible with the affected employee, outlining the reasons for your decision; I once spent three hours in a meeting with an employee I had to let go. The reason: as a leader, it's important to put yourself in that person's shoes and understand that you're dealing with a human on the other side.

  A leader's job is simple: make their employees shine. Someone who keeps taking the credit for their staff's work might rise quickly to the top, but won't have staying power because no one will respect them. High-performing employees will leave for greener pastures, leaving only low-performing ones who won't step up to the plate because they know their work won't get acknowledged.

* * *

Renowned Italian polymath Vilfredo Pareto first discovered the 80:20 rule when studying the distribution of money among the population in Italy in the early 1900s. He observed that 80 per cent of wealth in the country belonged to 20 per cent of the population. When he applied the same study to other nations, he surprisingly found similar results.[5] Today, this concept is named the 'Pareto Principle' after him.

This principle doesn't just apply to pecuniary distribution. Other mathematicians, sociologists, and economists have discovered similar ratios in different fields. For example, in fundraising, 80 per cent of the money raised is contributed by 20 per cent of the donors. In sports, the top 20 per cent of athletes receive 80 per cent of the rewards. And in business, 80 per cent of sales come from 20 per cent of your clients.

The Pareto Principle even comes into play in most companies. Your top 20 per cent employees probably contribute to 80 per cent of the firm's revenue.

How does this help in optimizing everyone's performance?

I'd imagine most management books would recommend that you focus on the top 20 per cent. I oppose this. Instead, a company will only succeed if the other 80 per cent elevate their performances. To me, it doesn't make much sense to only shine the spotlight on your top performers and leave everyone else to fend for themselves. That's how you breed discontent.

Most adults understand that career progression is dependent on hard work. In the different companies I've led, when I compare the top performers with the stragglers, the only difference is usually in the application of knowledge. From an intellectual and skills perspective, there is little difference.

Einstein once said that if you judge a fish by its ability to climb a tree, the fish will live its whole life believing it's stupid.

---

[5] https://en.wikipedia.org/wiki/Pareto_principle

Those in the bottom half of the 80 percent pool might just be applying their skills in a different area.

Your skill as a leader is in recognizing these small details and channelling their talent to a place where they can swim better.

4: Maintaining Distance with Friends and Enemies

It might sound ironic. After all, isn't being human about creating close bonds with your charges? The truth is a lot more complicated. Relationships, no matter how carefully treated, will always affect your work.

Not everyone will like you. It's a fact of life. If you go through your whole life trying to please everyone, ironically, you might end up alienating them instead. It becomes worse when you start managing or leading people. The hard decisions you have to make will probably displease or even anger your employees.

I'm not advocating for you to keep your enemies closer so that you can take pre-emptive strikes when they take action. Instead, I believe that being a good leader means understanding that there will be employees who don't like you, compartmentalising their emotions, and still advocating for them and developing their skills.

Treat them the same way you treat those who support you. People can discern when you display favouritism, even when it's subtle. The knock-on effects might take time, but are devastating. Your employees will first begin losing respect for you and your leadership. Soon, people will spend more time brown-nosing you instead of doing their best work. Eventually, the company's culture will change for the worse.

On the flipside, it's also important not to let friendships get in the way of leadership. It's one of the reasons why I believe that while you should be close to your employees, you shouldn't be too close such that your emotions cloud your decision-making process.

I learned this the hard way. When I led the Oceania region as a young thirty-eight-year-old leader, I had several subordinates who were far older than me. In my valiant attempt to get their approval and buy-in, I tried to become friends with them. They treated me with kids' gloves instead and kept their distance. Initially, I felt despondent. I thought they didn't have faith in my ability as a manager.

However, over time, I realized that they wanted to keep their work and personal lives separate. Their behaviour wasn't a knock against my ability, just a decision based on years of experience working with different leaders. I didn't have to gain their respect by being friends with them. All I had to do was become the best possible manager they ever had.

I've also had the shoe on the other foot before, too.

Previously, when I was the marketing director for MSD, I was interviewing multiple candidates for a role in my team. To my surprise, during one of the sessions, my high school classmate walked in. He was just as shocked as I was. I could see from his facial reaction that he wasn't expecting me on the other side of the conference table.

The conversation was stilted and jarring, but got better as time progressed. We hadn't seen each other in a while, so it was easier to maintain a professional distance. After the interview ended, I was conflicted. I objectively thought that he was the best fit for the role, but was concerned over how his hiring might be perceived by the others.

After wrestling with my emotions, I finally decided to hire him. I believed that he would be a great team contributor and was prepared to defend my decision. I also disclosed our connection to the HR department so that they knew of any possible conflicts of interest.

Fortunately, my high school friend also didn't try to capitalise on our existing relationship for his own benefit. He worked hard and proved himself, and when it was time to decide candidates for promotion, my friend had done enough to receive it without any whispers of favouritism from the other employees.

Ultimately, when your staff understands that they'll be treated fairly and objectively independent of their opinions of you as a leader, they'll perform at their most optimal level.

* * *

Many fear the impending AI revolution and whether their jobs will soon be taken over by robots with faster processing speeds and better knowledge. While we're only at the start, I believe there's still a long way to go before AI reaches a state where it can genuinely take over without any human intervention. Still, I understand the apprehension. Progress is always scary and does leave marks on the world. No one has any need now for a horse-riding cowboy.

But, I've never underestimated human ingenuity. The key is to double down on our humanity, a characteristic that AI can never grasp and one that'll extend your effectiveness as an employee and soon, a leader.

* * *

Questions to Ponder Over

1. How will the AI revolution affect your career and industry? And have you begun incorporating AI into your work?
2. What are some acts that you or your leaders have done that made a positive impact on everyone around you?
3. Do you believe you are in 20 per cent or 80 per cent of the employees in your company, according to the Pareto Principle?

Chapter Seven

The Secrets to Presentations That Will Impress Your Leaders

'Every time you have to speak, you are auditioning for leadership.'

—James C. Humes, author and former presidential speechwriter, in his book *Speak Like Churchill, Stand Like Lincoln.*

ChrisNotes

- Presentations are great ways to make deep and notable impressions on the people watching.
- Refrain from using too many words. No one likes reading long sentences on multiple slides.
- A serious presentation doesn't mean you cannot crack timely jokes or do something unexpected.

There's a video of me deep in the archives of my previous company and floating in the outer reaches of the Internet bouncing a blue balloon for a day. During one portion, I was keeping the blue balloon up in the air while working on a small presentation with a colleague. It might have looked silly to people watching, but it was memorable and cemented the message we were sending—living with Type 1 diabetes is trying to go through your daily life while constantly playing keepy-uppy with a balloon.

It would have been simpler to create a video of me talking to the camera and raising awareness about Type 1 diabetes. But I would have lost the audience within the first ten seconds. Instead, I thought: what did I want to see if I was the viewer? The answer was simple. I wanted to be entertained and informed.

Presentations Are about the Audience, Not You. Make It Relatable to Them

Being memorable and relatable—that's the key to capturing the audience's attention and a great presentation. Stories are a great way. I've given and sat in many multiple presentations, some great and others not so great, and I noticed that those with relatable stories are always more memorable.

Several years ago, I went on a whirlwind business trip, covering eight Asian countries in ten days. These included cities that I rarely visited, which meant that most of the staff there didn't relate to me. I had to create a connection quickly in the first few minutes of the town hall or risk losing them. My strategy was to start with a personal story for each country.

In Indonesia, my first slide in the presentation was a picture of Bandung city. I remember the quizzical looks in the crowd. I explained that during my MBA studies, I had a good friend and MBA classmate. Bandung was her hometown, so I visited the city with her during our holidays. The crowd warmed up immediately.

In the Philippines, I walked up the stage to the music of a popular 1978 Filipino folk rock classic called 'Anak' sang by

Freddie Aguilar. Everyone in the country knows it. My first slide was a picture of the singer and shared with the crowd that a long time ago, a singer crooned this tune at a singing competition, the Seoul International Song Festival. I was mesmerized and being an amateur singer, hunted down the lyrics and sang it while showering.

In Thailand, I started my presentation with a picture of a woman from the Karen Long Neck tribe. Formerly from Burma, many of them fled the country during times of unrest and crossed the border to Thailand seeking safe haven. Many of them have since settled there and raised families. During my university days, I minored in East Asian cultures and headed to the Golden Triangle, an area where the borders of Thailand, Laos and Myanmar meet, for a four-month assignment. My subject: the Karen Long Neck tribe.

In all of these instances, the memorable stories helped me to form instant connections with everyone in the crowd. They listened intently to every word I said afterwards.

Whether you're presenting to a big crowd or a room of decision makers, the tactics remain the same. Be memorable, relatable, and follow the tips below.

Use Language Suitable for the Audience

Many mask their nervousness or the presentation's deficiencies with jargon. Some also use it to show off their in-depth knowledge of a topic. The only thing that jargon does, however, is turn the audience off. As much as possible, use plain language and simple vocabulary. It's not about dumbing down the content and more about ensuring that everyone understands the messages you're transmitting. If you do need to present a difficult topic, using examples that a layman can understand to give context helps massively.

For example, I always use plain language during my town hall meetings when sharing how the company is doing. You won't hear financial jargon such as GAAP (generally accepted accounting principles) or EBITDA (earnings before interest, taxes, depreciation, and amortization) in my speeches because most don't truly understand what these acronyms mean. All they want to know is if they're getting a bonus.

Also, avoid generic statements in your presentation. These are sentences that are either obvious or place an entire group of people into one category. Business examples include (and I'm sure you must have listened to many of these during your career):

1. 'Diversity is important for innovation.' It's a motherhood statement that doesn't add anything new to the conversation.
2. 'Women and men must work together to achieve gender equality in the workplace.' While it has good intentions, it also doesn't push your presentation forward meaningfully. Instead, consider a more forceful statement such as men must do more to help achieve gender parity, to give an example.
3. 'Aim for low-hanging fruit.' Ah, a typical sentence I always hear in business strategy meetings.

For example, when giving financial updates on the company's performance, presentations should be catered to different employees. Ask yourself: 'Is this something the newest or most junior employees would understand?' Use analogies or examples to make data easily understood.

Take Note of Your Audience's Attention Span

Great language is futile if you cannot retain your audience's attention span. It's a perennial problem for any speaker.

Studies have discovered that people usually stop listening to a presentation after ten minutes. Their minds will begin to wander, and it's your job to retain them.

Some use visuals and videos (see point below) while others create some form of interaction with questions and props. A few also invite new speakers to change the pace and introduce something different to the presentation.

In 2018, I had to deliver a two-hour business presentation to over 5,000 employees in a large dimly lit stadium. The environmental conditions naturally made the audience sleepy and when you're in that state, you dread listening to a long and dry speech. I used all the tricks in the bag, including sharing compelling stories, using visually striking images in the deck and more. But attention spans will still wane, no matter how hard you try.

So, halfway through the presentation, I invited the audience to cast a vote: take a quick break, let's dance, or finish the session now. Most of them voted 'dance' because they were curious. Other leaders came out to dance on stage with me (rehearsed ahead of time, of course) and the audience joined in as well. It made everyone laugh, refreshed the audience, and brought the energy levels up again.

We powered through until the end.

Use As Many Visually Striking Images As Possible

One of my favourite examples for this point happened when I chaired a startup competition in 2021 in Medtronic. Titled the Medtronic APAC Innovation Challenge, it was the first such initiative we did and was wildly successful with over 300 applicants vying for collaborations with Medtronic valued at up to $200,000.

One of the participating founders was a former doctor who quit the practice to improve the medical products that physicians used in invasive procedures. He felt that more could be done to help both patients and doctors have better outcomes during surgeries.

The reason why I remembered him was because his first few slides were chock-full of incredibly graphic pictures of body parts in emergency room operations, all of which he took. He wanted to drive home the severity of the problem and explain how his solution minimized it. The doctor took a risk, but it paid off.

All of us remembered him and the work he was trying to achieve with his company, and crowned the doctor as one of the five winning startups.

Always Leave Room for Spontaneity

In 2011, I had an important presentation in front of 6,000 people. Just before I went on stage, my brother called me. He said that our father had passed away. I didn't have time to compose myself; it was my turn to be in the spotlight.

So, I went up and faced the audience, and I told them that I had just received the type of call that no one wants to receive. But, instead of being sad, I told the audience that I was glad Bayer's products extended my father's life by several months so that all of us in the family could spend a bit more time with him before he left this mortal coil. I told everyone in the audience that we weren't just selling pharmaceutical products; we were deepening connections.

My speech wasn't planned. I also didn't intend to take advantage of my personal loss for corporate gain. I only wanted to share a story close to me and explain how the work we were doing was helping other people lead better, more fulfilling lives. Most people can sense when you're disingenuous. Authenticity, even when spontaneous, that comes from the heart will make anyone listening relate better to you.

After I returned from the funeral, my team told me that employees rated my presentation the highest. It received a 100 percent satisfaction rate in the survey, which hadn't been achieved before.

Transform the Typical Q&A Session at the End into Part of Your Presentation

People usually spend the most time preparing for presentations and less time on the Q&A session at the end. But the latter is equally important. It is a chance to maintain control of the session and leave a deeper impression.

During the 1997 Korean Financial Crisis, we were discussing a company acquisition proposal. My aim was to convince the board of directors that it was a sound decision even if the current situation wasn't stable. I knew I would face two questions: one, whether South Korea was a good country to invest in; second, why should they invest in a country on the precipice of ruin.

I began my presentation with the first question and replied in the affirmative. The chairperson then asked me, 'Why would you invest $25 million in Korea?'

I replied, 'Honestly, if it was my own money, I wouldn't invest in Korea. But that's because I don't have so much liquidity. If I did, I would because in the long run, countries will not disappear.' Then, I went on to elaborate on the country's track record and its potential.

They agreed to invest the money.

Always anticipate the questions you'll get. Then, write them out at the start. This makes you stand out.

One of my previous organizations had gone through several rounds of restructuring. There was a sense of uncertainty and negative sentiment in the air, sparking tension between departments. People wondered, 'Why are there so many people in this department compared to other departments? What is their contribution to the company? Who's really driving revenue and who should be reaping the most benefit?' I needed to change people's mindsets.

Instead of sweeping these tough questions under the carpet, I invited employees to gather for an informal session with me. I addressed their questions at the start instead of allowing questions only at the end. This steered the presentation and showed the leadership team's willingness to be transparent. Employees appreciated the fact that we proactively acknowledged their concerns. Many understood and accepted the painful decisions that management had to make.

In these situations, many employees will always be left in the dark, which leaves them frustrated and angry. Imagine seeing you or your colleague being let go without any explanations beyond the usual financial spiel that companies love trotting out. Those who remain will still have dampened morale.

My session with them pre-empted this and ensured that the company didn't operate under a cloud of uncertainty.

Go through Your Slides with a Fine-Tooth Comb

I am extremely demanding with my presentation slides. I'll repeatedly comb through each slide and ask my team and myself for ways to make it more interesting. Remember that your audience, whether they are your staff or senior leaders, will tend to lose focus after a while. It's important to snap their attention back to you and your presentation.

Depending on your audience, you can also add some cheek to your presentation. During my time in South Korea, there was a rumour about me growing legs and running even though it sounded incredulous. Apparently, I had gone through four divorces and fathered children with multiple women. If you knew me as a friend, peer or manager, you would have laughed your head off. Instead of letting this rumour fester,

I confronted it head-on. I thought it was important to nip it in the bud. At one of my presentations, I put this statement in my first slide.

Chris Lee has been divorced four times and has children with multiple women.

I discussed it casually, refuted the rumours and shared the truth of my family. At the end, I mentioned that while I didn't mind being the topic of entertainment, it was important to have empathy. What if these rumours were about a female employee? Imagine how she would feel.

That slide and my brief and succinct explanation immediately doused the rumour flame, and made everyone sit up and listen. After all, presentations can be boring, especially for the viewer, and I wanted to accomplish two things with that slide: one, grab their attention and two, restore my reputation.

I'd imagine most leaders would either ignore the rumours. A few might even head towards the other end of the spectrum and threaten legal action. I thought it would be beneficial to reveal a few personal details so that my staff could relate to me. I also wanted to convey the idea that senior executives and leaders are human, too, and are just as badly affected by unsubstantiated rumours.

Two days later, I had a meeting with four senior union leaders. The main representative asked for a private chat with me and apologized. He was the one who had spread the rumour. I accepted his apology and told him I had no hard feelings.

Use Icebreakers

Everyone loves a good joke or a fun story. Even for serious presentations, an appropriate icebreaker at the beginning can warm the audience up and help you to build a connection with them. Test your icebreakers in front of a small group first to see if they are appropriate for the presentation you're about to give.

In 2014, I delivered a fifteen-minute presentation at the Asia Society's 2014 Diversity Leadership Forum in NYC on a serious topic—the difference in expectations of Asian Americans working at multinational companies.

To make the opening light and memorable, I began with a funny story of how a US immigration officer tried to communicate with an Asian traveller who did not speak English, which reminded me of my first entry into the country many years ago. It was something the audience could relate to and made them laugh. The organizers told me it was one of the highest-rated sessions at that event.

On another occasion at a startup competition, I had to sit through more than twenty presentations to shortlist a few winners. Most of the contestants tried to explain the technicalities of their innovations in a ten-minute pitch, but one stood out because he began with a personal story to grab everyone's attention.

Using a photo of himself in front of an 'Emergency Room', he spoke about his experience working in the ER and how painful it was for him to see patients suffering without a certain kind of treatment. That was his motivation for starting his company and why he planned to make a difference. Till today, I remember this founder. His story moved all the judges like myself and we selected him as one of the winners. Most of the finalists' products were excellent, but his ability to weave a compelling story set him apart from the rest.

Go Unscripted

A caveat: it might not work for everyone. But going without a script and presenting using points might be a good strategy if you're extremely familiar with your material. Some of the best presentations I've given have been unscripted. Your speech will be more natural and you can express your emotions more freely;

both are characteristics that will help you connect with your audience. No one likes listening to a robot.

You might stumble over some words or momentarily forget certain points, but being a natural and genuine speaker is far more important than being perfect. Going unscripted doesn't mean you don't prepare for your presentation, of course. In fact, you need to be doubly prepared and know your slides and material inside out. Then, you can go through your presentation effortlessly, no matter the questions you get or the audience you're giving it to.

* * *

Clear writing gives poor thinking nowhere to hide. Similarly, a great presentation gives life to the ideas in your head. The art of leadership is being able to convey your vision and direction to your team, and presentations help to achieve that.

Senior executives also look at a person's ability to give presentations. As James Humes said, 'Every time you have to speak, you're auditioning for leadership.' Give the best audition possible.

* * *

Questions to Ponder Over

1. What are your own presentation tricks that you like to use, too?
2. What was the best presentation that you've given in your life, whether in school, at the office or somewhere else?
3. What are some of your favourite presentations or speeches that you'd like to share?

Chapter Eight

The Art of Motivation, for Yourself and Your Team

'If your actions create a legacy that inspires others to dream more, learn more, do more and become more, then, you are an excellent leader.'

—Dolly Parton, singer and actor, quoted in a 1997 book titled *The Most Important Thing I Know*

ChrisNotes

- Your staff are the cogs that make the company move forward. Leaders who understand this, have won half the battle.
- Small and thoughtful gestures can go a long way in the workplace. Always look for opportunities to accomplish this.
- The simple act of remembering a person's name and addressing them by it the next time you see them is more impactful than you think.

In the late 1980s, I was scouted by Pepsico (the parent company that owned Pizza Hut, Taco Bell, Kentucky Fried Chicken, and Frito Lays snacks at that time) to join its internship programme.

I was in the middle of my MBA programme at the Thunderbird School of Global Management, at Phoenix, Arizona. Pepsi was looking for business students from the Asia-Pacific because it predicted that the Asian region would grow dramatically in the future. It wanted to position the organization to take advantage of this growth by grooming Asian talent who were already familiar with cultural and business nous in the region.

News of Pepsico's search circulated on my campus and I was excited because I was a perfect candidate—I understood East Asia, I could speak Korean, Japanese, and Chinese, and I had the requisite qualifications. So I applied for the position.

A few weeks later, I received the good news. Pepsico wanted to interview me for the position. If I passed this final round, I would start my business career in one of the biggest conglomerates in the world. The excitement I felt was immense, but it was quickly deflated when I discovered the massive hurdle. I had to fly to Pepsico's headquarters in Dallas, Texas, and as a student, flying there was a big financial burden. It was also impossible to drive a car down and turn it into a day trip because I didn't have enough time to squeeze the interview in while juggling classes. This was before the advent of Zoom, of course.

I was stuck in between a rock and a hard place, and feared that my dreams would dissipate into the wind. Then, I received a plane ticket from Pepsico in the mail. I was elated. But, more surprises were in store. When I went to the airport on the day of the flight, I was shocked when the check-in counter put me in first class. I was expecting an economy seat, but Pepsico happily paid three times more to fly me in comfort.

It was already dark when I arrived in Dallas due to the time difference. While clearing immigration, I was wondering if public transport was still available. To my utter disbelief, a man was waiting for me at the exit, holding a sign with my name and the words, 'Welcome to Pepsico'. Then, he took my luggage and led me to a waiting limousine. I was beginning to think that the company had mistook me, a lowly student that wasn't even an intern, to be a hotshot executive.

The third surprise happened at the end of the ride. I was expecting a motel. Instead, the driver dropped me off at the Ritz-Carlton Dallas, a five-star hotel, before telling me that he would pick me up at nine the next morning for the interview.

I showed up at the lobby bright and early, ready to tackle the interview. True to his word, the driver showed up on time, wished me good morning and whisked me off to the Pepsico headquarters. When I arrived, I recognized the face waiting for me. He was the human resources manager who was recruiting potential interns at my school several months ago. He greeted me warmly and then led me into the building.

Over the next several hours, several executives from different departments interviewed me. It was an admittedly tiring affair and I was glad when the final interview wrapped up. Pepsico didn't shoo me away immediately. Instead, a representative took me for a tour around their large headquarters. What struck me were the happy faces of all the employees I met. They all seemed to enjoy working for the company. It made me also hope that I passed the gruelling interview rounds so that I could be a part of Pepsico. The limousine was still waiting for me after I completed everything.

The extent that Pepsico went for me, a young man who was neither an important person in the company nor even an employee, moved me greatly. Till this day, thirty years later, I have taken this lesson to heart and tell this story to anyone who wants to know how to motivate people and groom ambassadors. You don't need to spend millions on marketing campaigns. All you need is to treat anyone who interacts with your company with the greatest respect. That's how you create motivation.

My short visit to Pepsico and subsequent internship taught me the importance of several things, including the four mantras that I'll be sharing in the next few pages.

* * *

1. Look for Opportunities to Make People Feel Important

It's a practice I started when I was at MSD and something I continued even when I was at Medtronic, and now at VentureBlick. Every few days, when my team tells me that we have a fresh batch of employees going through the onboarding process, I'd make time to pay them a visit.

I don't prepare any speeches or materials. My only aim is to introduce myself to them and share that I'm prepared to ask any questions they have. New employees are generally full of queries about company revenue, internal regulations, welfare systems and more, and I do my best to answer each and every question. This session is usually done like those Q&A sessions at the end of every presentation. It's a lot more informal, of course. My aim is to make them feel like they're part of a big family.

I've been thrown surprisingly probing and sensitive questions, including some who ask about retrenchments or rumours that they've heard in the media. My approach, and one I highly recommend to everyone, is to answer with honesty and dignity. Many people are used to leaders hemming and hawing, and giving an answer that beats around the bush without addressing the question. So, my frankness is always refreshing. I've always believed that you can be honest without being cruel.

I don't have all the answers, naturally. So, for questions that I'm unsure about, I'll tell them to approach the head of a relevant department and mention my name.

Once, a new hire even asked what my salary was. A bold question, to say the least, and one I was thoroughly unprepared for. Instead of giving him a rough figure or telling him that it was confidential, I said, 'I'll show you in person if you are really curious.' The next day, I brought my pay stub and showed it to him. An unconventional move, but I wanted to demonstrate to him and the rest of the people present that I was sincere and always kept to my promises.

Making your colleagues and staff feel that they matter and are important to the organization foster trust and teamwork. It also generates happiness, a core component of any well-oiled company.

* * *

In the first few months of my stint as the managing director of Bristol-Myers Squibb in Australia, a journalist requested to interview me. News of my unconventional management style in Korea had spread around the office, to the point that even news organizations became interested. I thought the interview was a good opportunity to promote the company as a thought leader in the pharmaceutical industry, so I agreed to it.

After showing the writer around our office, we sat down for a chat. Most of the questions were cursory and expected, but one stood out for me. The reporter asked, 'The performance of management can be boiled down to one aspect: sales. How do you plan to increase sales in the future?' On the surface, it might seem rudimentary. However, I thought this was the perfect chance to explain my leadership mantra.

I told him. 'I think there are two ways to increase sales. One is to squeeze your employees as much as possible to achieve their goals. The other is to get them to work hard. I believe in the latter method. How do you convince them to work hard? You make them happy. Once they are happy, they will work hard and the company's productivity will naturally increase.'

I shared an example of my time as a middle manager in my twenties. During that period, numerous companies tried to poach me and many dangled tempting offers in front of me. However, each time I received an offer, my boss would ask me for twenty-four hours to convince me to stay. I always said yes. Then, within a day, a senior executive would reach out to me and share how important I was to the company. These overtures always moved me and convinced me to stay.

'I apply the same practice now in whatever company I'm in,' I said. 'I've told all my managers that if an employee whom we want to keep hands in a resignation letter, we ask them for at least twenty-four hours. Then, I'll carve time from my schedule to have a conversation with the staff the next day to try and convince them to stay.'

When this interview ran in the papers, it was all that the employees could talk about for several weeks. They became more motivated after knowing that the company's leaders had their backs and valued their output. I'm glad to report that productivity also improved.

2. Value Your Employees

It might seem like a throwaway line, but I find that many companies never walk the talk. The best example: the hybrid working debate that is still raging on months after the Covid-19 pandemic has officially ended. It's fair to say that many employees favour a hybrid working model because it saves them time that is no longer spent dressing up or commuting to work. Many companies, however, are increasingly forcing their staff to return to the office. There is no right or wrong answer, but it clearly shows that many senior management don't listen if what they're hearing doesn't suit them.

This reminds me of an experiment I carried out during my time at Bristol-Myers Squibb Australia. At that point, the government-mandated number of working hours per week was 37.5. On average, that's about 7.5 hours every day, assuming one works from Monday to Friday. I upended the model and instituted an official guideline. I told the company that I didn't care when they came in as long as they clocked 37.5 hours of work in the office. If someone chose to work twelve hours on Monday, Tuesday and Wednesday, they could have Thursdays and Fridays off.

The employee had free rein over how they wanted to manage their time. For example, they could come in at 6 a.m., take a two-hour lunch break, and work until 9 p.m.

My aim was simple: I wanted the employees to know that the company valued their time and the work they did, and that quality was more valuable than quantity. Everyone has different schedules. Parents would probably prefer to work shorter hours in a day to spend more time with their children while singles, I'd imagine, would rather have a longer weekend to pursue personal goals.

It wasn't easy. Many managers opposed this move and cited numerous reasons, including the inability to observe their staff or check on the work. I pressed on with my proposal and told management that they shouldn't check how long employees work, but how effective they are at their jobs. Competent workers shouldn't be punished for being able to complete tasks quicker than their counterparts.

After a successful three-month pilot trial in the Victoria office in Melbourne, this scheme extended to all the Bristol-Myers Squibb offices in Australia.

Even after the success of this experiment, many still asked if I made the right decisions and I heard remarks from senior executives that they hoped it would fail. But, productivity improved and I could feel a lighter mood in the office each time I came to work. Smiles were omnipresent, too.

* * *

Something I've never understood is the reluctance of senior leaders to spend the company's excess budget on their employees. It could be something as simple as company-wide meals or even discretionary bonuses to help with rising costs of living. However, I've witnessed multiple instances of company executives blowing huge amounts of cash on lavish meetings or first-class seats during work travels.

I once knew of a personal assistant to a senior business leader who was retiring. She had worked for him for over fifteen years. You'd think that such a long period of service would mean something to the leader and he would prepare something special for her. On her last day, he gave an envelope to her containing a gift. The gift? A $50 food voucher expiring the month after.

In contrast, while I'm not the paragon of generosity, I've always believed in giving as much as I can to the people who make my work and personal lives easier. I once had an incredibly hard working secretary who followed me from company to company. She knew me inside out and could anticipate my needs even before I voiced them.

She decided to quit after some time to enjoy her golden years. To show my appreciation, I bought a Louis Vuitton purse for her after noticing that her own wallet was falling apart. I also paid for everyone who came for her farewell lunch. I never intended to broadcast these acts, but people knew and talked about it.

We don't even have to look far to see examples of companies valuing their employees' contributions. In early 2023, Singapore-based F&B company Paradise Group made the news for giving out a Rolex watch to ninety-eight long-serving employees, regardless of their position.[6] All of them had worked over a decade with the operator. Several hundred more were given other long-service gifts, including a gold bar.

Paradise Group mentioned that the anniversary celebrations cost them over $2 million. I'm certain the goodwill they generated from this generous act will be worth even more. I remember reading multiple positive news articles and comments about this; I even jokingly wondered if they were hiring and looking for a healthcare professional.

3. Protect Your Employees and They Will Return the Favour

Several decades ago, when I was the sales and marketing director at MSD, I faced a tricky situation. It was a bright and beautiful morning, but my mood didn't reflect the weather. I was urgently looking for a sales staff regarding an important matter, but he was nowhere to be found.

When I searched for his counterpart, I realized he, too, was missing. Initially, I didn't think too much of it, thinking that the both of them had gone out for sales meetings and neglected to inform me. Shortly after, however, the wife of one of them called me. She was upset and I could hear her loud, heaving sobs on the phone. He hadn't come home the night before and she was deathly afraid that something bad had happened to him.

My first thought was to calm the wife down. Then it hit me. Both sales managers had obnoxious drinking habits. They would

---

[6] https://www.straitstimes.com/singapore/98-rolex-watches-given-to-long-serving-employees-of-paradise-group

consume alcohol late into the night and drag their subordinates along with them, even though many of them didn't like it.

I reassured the wife by saying that her husband actually had drinks with me till late and he fell asleep at my place. 'We went to work together, but I had to go for a business trip and I neglected to call you and let you know that your husband is with me. He's in an important meeting now, which is probably why he's not answering the phone,' I said.

Relieved, she hung up the phone. I decided to investigate. My first stop was to the office cubicles to ask the staff if they had been drinking with their bosses the night before. I didn't even need to open my mouth; the late nights hung clearly on their tired eyes like a trapeze artist swinging from the beam.

I confirmed my suspicions by asking one of them if they had a late business meeting the previous night. He nodded.

After lunch, the sales managers finally showed up, walking into my room and reeking of alcohol. I could see the shame and sheepishness on their faces. They probably thought they were going to get chewed out.

Instead, I calmly asked them if their mornings had gone well. 'I also got a call from one of your wives. She was incredibly upset, but I told her that you were in an important meeting and was out with me the previous night till late,' I continued. Their faces turned a deeper shade of red.

'Don't worry, I will close one eye regarding your morning absence.' I didn't bring up their late-night drinking session.

A few days later, the same sales managers asked me out for lunch and apologized for their behaviour. They were prepared for a massive scolding, but were touched at my balanced reaction. They also shared that their threshold for drinking had dropped over the years, but still thought they could hold their liquor. That night drove home the point that they couldn't anymore.

Their remorse convinced me that no further punishment needed to be meted out. The humiliation they suffered was more than enough for them to understand that their behaviour was uncalled for. I've always believed that you should treat your colleagues and employees like adults instead of children that need to be chided.

Overnight, their behaviours changed. They stopped their nightly drinking habits, only indulging in a tipple once or twice a month.

The typical managerial reaction would have been to fire them on the spot for their unprofessionalism. Their behaviour warranted this drastic action. But, I wanted to show magnanimity, believing that it would pay off in the long run. When employees know that their superiors will protect them through thick and thin, they'll work harder and be happier.

4. Remember Your Employees' Personal Details

It might seem trite and oft-repeated in business blogs, but I cannot emphasise enough the importance of memorising your employees' details such as their names or personal details. In fact, I strongly believe that it's a lot more valuable for bosses to remember the names of their employees rather than the other way around. It is hard work, but nothing worthwhile ever comes easy.

This habit was ingrained in me because of one of my superiors in MSD. Because of my impressive sales performance, I was assigned to headquarters. The company had the practice of circulating the names and personal details of new hires to everyone, including the CEO, via email.

There were over hundreds of thousands of employees in the office back then, so I wasn't expecting to be remembered. Several days later, as I was taking the elevator to work, the CEO stepped in, too. I remained quiet, not wanting to intrude into his privacy.

A few minutes after the door closed, he turned to me and said, 'You're Chris Lee who recently got promoted to senior manager, right? Good job.' I was moved that he remembered me and my promotion and awed that he could even remember the small details, all achieved without us having even met.

It's simple to discern my race or name based on my appearance and my name tag, but the CEO oversees several hundreds of thousands employees, yet still remembers me from a simple email.

This episode spurred me to work harder. When I began my leadership journey, I made sure to memorise my employees' names and small details about them to demonstrate that I valued and appreciated their work.

Even till today, I treat my employees like my customers. Client interaction requires service excellence. I set the same high standards when I manage my employees. That's a core component in motivating your staff to demand high standards from themselves and their peers.

* * *

Your people can sense when you're being disingenuous. It's not enough that you just do something good once. You have to think about them daily and tweak your behaviour to incorporate them into your personal and business lives. Chinese philosopher Lao Tzu once said, 'Watch your thoughts, they become your words; watch your words, they become your actions; watch your actions, they become your habits; watch your habits, they become your character; watch your character, it becomes your destiny.'

Dozens, if not hundreds of books, are written for leaders to understand how to manage, motivate and encourage their followers, or employees. But many of these so-called words of wisdom can be distilled to this mantra: your staff are your first customers.

Begin with the small things. Once, after I took over the country division of a company, I replaced the old and rickety coffee machine from the pantry with the newer, shinier version sitting in my room. I put the older one back in my room, telling the team that I wasn't fussy with my daily cup of joe and felt that the new coffee machine could be put to better use by everyone else. It was a small act, but it showed everyone that I always put them first. Remember Lao Tzu's words as you build your team and company. It's all about your thoughts. That is servant leadership in a nutshell.

* * *

Questions to Ponder Over

1. When was the last time a boss or leader made you feel like you were valued for your work and contributions?
2. Could you share with me one incident with your boss going the extra mile for you that has stuck in your mind?
3. What would you do differently as a leader of your company, if given the chance?

Chapter Nine

Why I Believe in Servant Leadership? (Going the Extra Mile)

'Leadership is the art of motivating a group of people to act toward achieving a common goal.'
—Susan Ward, entrepreneur, writing for *The Balance Business* blog on 27 January 2023

ChrisNotes

- There are many forms of leadership. The most effective is the one that puts people first.
- Your staff are adults, not children. Trust and empower them to do their jobs.
- The era of authoritative leadership is long gone. People no longer respond to threats. Instead, learn to collaborate.

There are several leadership styles, but the most common are:

- **Traditional leadership:** The top-down model that sees leaders at the top of the totem pole barking orders down to the people below them.

- **Democratic leadership:** Instead of a person deciding everything, this style involves a group of employees casting votes and deciding the way forward together.
- **Laissez-faire leadership:** Employees have full autonomy over their work and don't require approval from the bosses. The company operates on the basis that everyone is acting in its best interests.
- **Servant leadership:** Rather than being at the top of the totem pole, like traditional leadership, the CEO or founder is at the bottom, working in service of the staff.

Author Robert Greenleaf first conceptualized the idea of a servant leader in his 1970 essay titled 'The Servant as a Leader'. Greenleaf felt that the authoritarian style of leadership he saw in American companies was no longer working and detrimental to business. Several decades later, consultant Larry Spears expanded on this concept, citing that servant leaders demonstrated these ten qualities:[7]

- Listening
- Empathy
- Healing
- Awareness
- Persuasion
- Conceptualization
- Foresight
- Stewardship
- Commitment to people's growth, and
- Building community

---

[7] https://www.spearscenter.org/46-uncategorized/136-ten-characteristics-of-servant-leadership

As I rose through the ranks, this style of leadership resonated with me, even if I didn't know its name then. To me, the mark of a successful leader is one who grooms his or her employees to grow, excel and potentially become leaders themselves.

It's also about doing the right thing for your staff even when they're not around. One of the ways that you can tell if someone is genuinely nice is to observe what they do when they think no one is watching. The best example is something I like to call the shopping cart test. Ubiquitous in supermarkets and big box stores such as Ikea, these carts are either free or cost the user a minimal deposit—usually a dollar coin that can only be retrieved when the cart is returned.

The dilemma comes after users have lugged their items to the car. What do they do with the cart? It costs them time and effort to return the cart to a designated area, and with no benefit to themselves—except perhaps getting their inconsequential dollar back. The only ones who benefit are the next people using the cart.

Sometimes, I joke that the best way to judge society is not only by how they treat their animals, but whether they return their shopping carts.

It reminds me of a management-only meeting I had at one of my previous companies. During these sessions, I don't like to say much and only chime in when my opinion is needed or if I think that we're making a terrible decision for the organization. It felt like the latter during this session. The context: the executives were discussing a possible trip to Hawaii to meet with the founder for a strategy and management meeting. For those in the room, it sounded perfect—mixing work and pleasure in one of the most beautiful locations in the world.

There was just one problem though. The company had just gone through a restructuring exercise, so spending a large sum of money on a management retreat felt extremely tone-deaf to me.

I felt that it would alienate the employees, many of whom had been told that there would be no bonuses or increments because of the uncertain macroeconomic environment. Unfortunately, it seemed that no one had similar sentiments. Everyone was excited. I kept quiet. When it finally came time to put this idea to the vote, incidentally, I was the last one to cast it. All the other executives enthusiastically said yes. During my turn though, I expressed my thoughts and said that 'it was the stupidest idea I've heard' before explaining why I felt this way.

There was silence in the room. I could see everyone's eyes trained on me and you could hear the cogs grinding in their heads. Finally, one person agreed out loud. Slowly, everyone else fell in line, giving their assent. Some even remarked that the original idea shouldn't even have been entertained in the first place. There's an allegory in there about groupthink, but that's for another book.

The trip to Hawaii fleetingly disappeared into the wind. The founder flew to us instead for that meeting. Imagine the negative press that the company would have accrued.

Servant leadership encourages you to always think of your employees, even if it might cost you in the short term. It's about having faith in your people. I've shared several anecdotes in this chapter showing the magical things that can happen when you trust your employees. Of course, there will be times when someone will take advantage of the goodness of your heart, but the good far outweighs the bad. Being a servant leader has also greatly benefited my career. When you make your employees look good, they will, in turn, go above and beyond in their work, which will ultimately benefit you.

1. Helping an Employee in Debt

When I was leading Bristol-Myers Squibb Korea, I once received a legal note. The court had applied to garnish 50 per cent of an employee's monthly wage, bonuses and any potential severance pay, excluding the minimum cost of living designated in Korea at that time. It was a large amount and one that I could not help the employee with.

I didn't ask him what happened. But he was badly affected. His productivity plummeted and he came to the office daily with a forlorn face. It was obvious that he had lost the motivation to work. Naturally, his performance sunk to the depths and senior management discussed the possibility of letting him go.

I thought about it for quite a while. Before the court order, this employee posted stellar performances month after month. I thought it would be unfair for the company to leave him high and dry when he had devoted so much time and energy to the organization so that it could be successful.

After much deliberation, I increased the employee's remuncration and provided the court with his severance pay to help pay down his debt. It was an unusual move, but I believed that if we went the extra mile for him, he would be doubly motivated.

My hunch was right.

The employee was extremely touched by our actions. He was worried about his living conditions and revealed that his house had been on the brink of foreclosure. The infusion of cash came at the perfect time.

After that day, he no longer came to the office with sadness in his eyes. The pep in his step returned and his productivity not only improved, but exceeded his previous efforts. He was a man reborn.

Everyone's life unfolds in unexpected ways. Occasionally, some might face difficulty that they might not be comfortable with sharing. As a manager or leader, it is our responsibility to care for those under us and note how they feel. An empowered employee will be a revelation for the bottom-line.

2. Helping an Employee Even after They've Left

How far should a leader take care of his or her employees? It's normal, especially in smaller organizations, for managers to build close bonds with their staff. However, it's usually hard, if not impossible, for both to become close friends due to the nature of the relationship. That doesn't mean, however, that you should not help them if you can.

I once had a former subordinate who reached out to me after I had left the company. He was in trouble and didn't know who else to turn to. I was based in Australia at that time and my ex-employee was in Korea.

According to the email he had sent to me several days before, he had made an unintentional mistake that placed him and the company in an awkward position. The organization wanted to dismiss him with immediate effect, but he fought back, stating that it was unfair because he didn't do it intentionally. It was a losing battle, of course. The firm had a lot more resources than him.

This man had been a valuable and hardworking subordinate, so I wanted to help him out. After meeting him in Korea and hearing the full story, I flew to the US headquarters to meet with the senior executives. I was still on talking terms with many of them, so they readily agreed to have a chat when I told them I wanted to discuss this issue.

The organization had begun assembling a legal team and I told them that I felt it was a big mistake. 'Even if you win the case, this man will leave the company on a terribly sour note. If he remains in the pharmaceutical industry, which is more than likely, he will spread stories about the firm that will put you in a bad light,' I elaborated. The management noted my concerns. I had done all I could.

Finally, after some time, I received word that the employee had resigned and would be paid during his notice period.

I breathed a sigh of relief when I heard that and then helped him to get another role within my network.

I didn't need to hold out my hand and drag him back up to solid ground after he had been pushed off the precipice. But I knew that it was the right thing to do. Till today, we remain in touch.

3. Trusting Your Employees Even if They Pass Disparaging Remarks

You cannot make everyone happy. This rings especially true when you're managing a team. There will be people who will be displeased with your decision, the way you run the organization or even just how you dress and look. Ultimately, you cannot let your staff's feelings affect your decision-making process.

You can't let the gossip and negativity get to your heart, too. During my tenure at Bristol-Myers Squibb Korea, I found out about a staff who spread rumours about me to anyone who would listen. Gossip is commonplace in any large organizations, but these untruths were particularly vicious. I remained calm and even reflected on my behaviour, wondering if I had done something to trigger this behaviour.

One day, this rumourmonger applied to be posted overseas. It's a coveted opportunity and only the best-performing employees went on these assignments. His request landed on my desk. I stared at his form for several minutes, swaying between approving the request and rejecting it. Finally, I gave my seal of approval. The man was a high performer and deserved the posting. I didn't want to let my personal opinions colour his future.

Unfortunately, even during his overseas assignment, he continued spreading rumours about me. I never thought to confront him about it because I didn't think it would achieve anything.

Unlike the numerous other anecdotes in the previous chapters, this story doesn't have a satisfactory ending. But, I thought it was important to highlight that servant leadership means always doing the right thing, even if you don't want to.

I gave a second recommendation to this employee later in his career because his performance deserved it, and as far as I'm aware, he has continued spreading rumours about me, unaware that I was responsible for his rise up the corporate ladder.

Someone once asked me why I still continued to display magnanimity to this man when he didn't deserve it. My answer was simple. 'I am his leader.'

4. Prioritizing Junior Employees Over Senior Ones

Asian cultures place huge emphasis on seniority. The young, able-bodied generation tend to give a lot of respect to the elderly. There's a Chinese saying that goes, 'I have eaten more salt than you have rice.' It's a proverb that emphasises the gulf in experience between an older person and his or her young buck. This culture also bleeds into the workplace. Older or more senior employees usually have more of the spotlight because of their perceived depth of knowledge that can only be gleaned through years and years of experience.

I have a different take. I usually give more attention to my junior staff. When they email me, my replies are longer and have more heft to them. If any of them approach me voluntarily, I always put aside my work temporarily and listen to them.

My reason is simple: senior staff already spend more time with me because they have to get approval for projects or conduct presentations. The less experienced employees will usually shun the limelight. They will also have to gather their courage to talk to me, so I know that if they do, it must be a serious topic. They also usually appreciate the time spent with me a lot more than those in middle or upper management.

In the same vein, I usually decline lunch and dinner invitations from my subordinates because I want to maintain that separation in and out of the office. I also want to respect their work–life balance. But, if junior employees many levels below me ask me out for a meal, I happily accept. I want to show them that I value their time and bravery. While eating, our conversations can range from work to culture, but I always find time to pick their brains for ideas and listen to their feedback about the office. They can give insight you won't hear from others.

To me, this is the easiest form of servant leadership you can easily put into practice.

5. Why Servant Leadership Pays Off?

Finding talent is already hard. Keeping them is almost impossible. Such talents are naturally sought after by many and it's inevitable that your top performers will be poached by organizations with bigger budgets and better projects. While you and your company might not be able to compete on depth and scale, you can convince talented people to join you on the strength of your management style. And servant leadership lends itself well to this.

In my decades in management, I've seen many employees who join a company because of a good leader. Everyone wants a competent boss who can lead them to success. Beyond intelligence and capability, employees want someone who has their best interests at heart.

I first joined Bristol-Myers Squibb Korea when it was just founded and needed to hire staff and management. This was before the rise of the Internet, so the best way to advertise your job openings was through the newspaper. At that time, Bristol-Myers Squibb wasn't well-known in the country. Many believed that we were a small digital company. Others even thought we were a multi-level marketing firm. A simple Google search now would easily shed light on the company's business, but again, this was an era before the World Wide Web.

However, my name was widely known in the pharmaceutical industry. I had risen through the ranks in MSD and helmed several teams before leaving MSD Korea after seven years. So, when I put up that job advertisement in the newspaper, a large number of employees from MSD Korea, many of whom had worked with me in some capacity, sent in their resumes. The avalanche shocked me, but warmed my heart, too. I was glad that I measurably impacted their careers and lives.

I wasn't under any illusion that Bristol-Myers Squibb in Korea could topple MSD. We were minnows compared to them. In the global market, MSD was twice the size of Bristol-Myers Squibb, too.

However, the employees who applied to join didn't care about this. When my hiring team asked them why they wanted to join, all of them mentioned my name. It wasn't because I was kind and supported them with my heart. Those were a given. Instead, they felt empowered by my trust in them in the previous company. They wanted to succeed together again as a team together with a leader whom they believed in.

* * *

I'm a big believer in empowerment. Artist and inventor Leonardo da Vinci once said, 'Poor is the pupil who does not surpass his master.' In my career, I've never wanted followers. Instead, I've always sought to build leaders and mavericks who could go on to achieve great things and build a resume that far surpasses mine.

That is what servant leadership is all about. We are all leaders in one way or another, whether it's in the office managing a team, at home building a family, or even with friends when deciding dinner plans. All of us work in service for one another and the sooner we realize and accept that, the more fulfilling our office and personal lives will be.

* * *

Questions to Ponder Over

1. What is your favourite leadership quote that you remember to this day? And how do you apply it in your life?
2. What is your own approach to leadership? Describe it in plain language.
3. When was the last time you went an extra mile for someone, whether it was a friend, colleague or employee? How did that make you feel?

Chapter Ten

The Differences in Leading a Big Organization vs Small Startup

I used to have a driver and car when I visited Korea for work during my days leading large pharmaceutical companies. Now, at VentureBlick, I take the subway. It took me a while to get used to the train system, but I'm quite the expert now. I can even tell you the exact spot you need to stand on the platform so that the train door stops directly in front of you.

It's a drastic lifestyle change. But I have embraced it. The subway is just one of the many adjustments I've had to make to get VentureBlick off the ground. I admit that it was tough in the beginning. After over three decades of leading large organizations, I became used to several privileges. All of that disappeared immediately the moment I stopped representing a multinational corporation. I am not resentful. I have learnt a lot. If anything, these incidents have made me even more determined to make VentureBlick a success.

I've had to learn quickly. Entrepreneurship is a different kettle of fish when you're sailing in a small dinghy instead of a large boat. But there are also benefits. You're more agile, can learn fast from mistakes, and have the ability to pivot quickly.

Here are several goals I've sent, and lessons I've learned, along the way.

Generating the First $100k Revenue as a Startup is the Hardest Goal You'll Achieve

When you're new, no one believes in you. It's ironic, but everyone wants to be the second person, not the first, to give you a shot. For many, being first means taking on unnecessary risk, all of which can be mitigated by letting someone else try it out first and handle the growing pains. Then, as the second mover, you reap the rewards of a more stable, battle-tested system. That's why I believe it's far easier for an MNC to earn $1 billion than a startup to bring in its first $100,000 in revenue.

When you're running the former, people tend to give you their flowers. They also swing open their doors and welcome you with open arms because of the strength of your company's brand. I also had a large team that would help me with daily administrative tasks so that I could focus on making decisions.

Life, and business, is vastly different when you run a startup. For example, the branch manager of a local bank in Korea used to approach me immediately when I entered his premises. I would even consider us acquaintances. Now, after leaving the corporate world and running VentureBlick, the same man remains in his office when I step into the bank. He does acknowledge me with a nod, but I have to take a ticket and join the queue.

In the early stages of building the startup, I also met with several of my close business contacts and shared VentureBlick's mission with them. Many of them supported my idea and briefly said in passing that they would support me when the firm is up and running.

When I approached them again after VentureBlick was finally running, I experienced rejection after rejection. Once I conducted forty pitches in a row to government agencies, potential investors, and other relevant people. All of them said no to me. While they were supportive on paper, the truth is revealed when the rubber hit the road. The more I faced these scenarios, the more I understood the problems that several of the healthcare startups we support are facing.

On the flipside, I also regularly have serendipitous encounters with former employees while walking the streets in Korea and Singapore. They smile when they see me. Some even take a huge bow. It's slightly embarrassing since I'm no longer their boss, but it feels nice to be remembered and know that many of them still hold me in high regard.

Once, a former employee was incredibly elated when I ran into her in Korea. She shared how she had benefited greatly after I sponsored her MBA programme—when we met, she had just graduated six months ago—and helped her with a difficult situation.

I take all of these positive and negative incidents in my stride. They remind me to behave consistently and treat everyone the same way, no matter our titles, positions or situations in life.

Business is slightly easier now after completing a few major deals, but I'll never forget that first six months.

The First Several Hires in Your Startup Can Make or Break the Company

An MNC can shrug off the devastating effects of a bad hire relatively easily. The contagion is usually limited to a small area and the boss can clean it up with the help of several trusted employees. A startup doesn't have the same fortune. One rotten apple can infect the rest and sabotage your company before it can even get off the ground.

Unfortunately, the allure of working in an MNC trumps the idea of joining a startup. There is supposed stability, larger resources and a well-oiled process in place. The brand name of the MNC also helps.

It's one of the reasons why I take my time with hiring. It's harder to find good people willing to roll the dice by joining a startup. That doesn't mean that there aren't great employees out there in the wild. There are several; we just have to be patient and find them. In a small team, how well (or not) one of my team members is doing can easily affect the sentiments of everyone else.

I also spend a longer period of time with prospective candidates to ensure that they not only have the right skills, mindset and drive for the company, but have great chemistry with the rest. I owe the team a good culture and a bright future. The last thing I want is to let them down.

Sometimes, I make mistakes. It might be a case of a bad fit, a miscommunication about the job's expectations, or the realization that they are better suited for the rigid structure of an MNC. In these cases, I have to make the difficult decision of letting them go. It's never easy. But, to be a good leader, you must do it to improve both your company's and the affected employee's situation.

There have been cases when the departure has been less than pleasant. Still, I always believe in taking the bull by its horns. I acknowledge their courage and the fact that they took the risk to join me. Then, I explain the reasons behind my decision and take time to ensure that the separation is amicable. Finally, I try to ensure that their last memory of the company is good with a farewell lunch and a gift. It's the least I can do.

Even when you've put together the best possible team, the work doesn't end there. Previously, in large companies, I admittedly didn't feel the same sense of ownership and accountability that I have now with VentureBlick. I even dream about the company now; I rarely, if ever, did in my previous roles.

People often tell me that it must be nice to be my own boss and have the freedom and creativity to do whatever I like. While it's true that I can try out new things that no one has done before and test to see if it works, without needing to get approval or lobby for support, I'm still accountable to my team. I owe it to them to make this venture a success. It is my constant reminder, my burden, and my motivation.

Rejection Is Extremely Common in a Startup

I'm used to hearing the word 'no' now. Before VentureBlick, I had never been rejected before in a professional capacity. It's strange, but true. I had the backing of a large organization behind me and that gave people confidence. The company on my name card meant something. I no longer have that now.

When you're new, very few are willing to give you a chance. Even more will refuse to reconnect with you on a professional level. When I was leading the Asia-Pacific region during my time in different healthcare companies, a hospital I regularly visited always rolled out the red carpet. There were flowers, photo opportunities, and more. I never had to make appointments. Now, the same hospital routes me to a personal assistant who checks the calendars before slotting me in for a business visit. The preferential treatment is stark and overwhelming.

The professional contacts I've made over the decades who clamoured to see me when I was in large MNCs also regularly avoid me at first. It takes repeated tries for me to secure a meeting and when I finally meet them, some tell me bluntly that they thought I was asking for money. Initially, I was disappointed, but have now realized that it's their professional personality.

You must stay positive in the face of overwhelming rejection and believe in your idea to the point of insanity. It took me a while to adjust my expectations. Now, I like to tell myself that those who don't believe or agree with me are wrong. I also use rejection to enhance my offerings and make tweaks, if needed, to my business model. Then, I move on to the next target. The world is big and there will be more opportunities.

Most startups are building a product or service that's disrupting a current method of doing things. In the case of VentureBlick, we're changing the way healthcare startups raise funds. Today, early-stage med- and pharma-tech companies have trouble getting off the ground because of exorbitant R&D costs and a field dominated by large legacy players. VentureBlick matches these startups to medical investors, who will ultimately become their customers. This solves their funding and market fit challenges, and validates their proposed solution.

My decades spent in the field made me realize this was an issue, which was I believe that VentureBlick will plug this gap. That's why I was initially confused when the first few venture capitalists I met either didn't understand the idea or doubted our model. One even asked me, 'So, what is the problem?'

I am reminded of Airbnb's rocky beginnings. In 2008, co-founders Brian Chesky, Nathan Blecharczyk, and Joe Gebbia sought to raise $150,000 for its online short-term homestay marketplace. The trio approached twelve investors. All of them turned the group down. One of the rejection emails Chesky received wrote:

'Hi Brian,

I apologize for the delayed response. We've had a chance to discuss internally and unfortunately don't think this is the right opportunity for [redacted] from an investment perspective. The potential market opportunity did not seem large enough for our required model.'[8]

---

[8] https://qz.com/452185/the-rejection-letters-of-early-round-investors-who-passed-on-airbnb

Just over a decade later, in 2022, Airbnb recorded a revenue of US$8.4 billion. The investor who wrote that email is certainly eating crow.

Stories like Airbnb are common and give me strength that VentureBlick's model is just not yet understood in several quarters of the venture capital world, many of whom don't understand healthcare as intimately as I do.

I believe we're on the right track. Since VentureBlick's inception in September 2022, we've grown to nearly fifty employees in seven countries and have over 1,000 advisors across the globe. We've also attracted over 700 startups from seventy countries seeking help with their solutions. Four of them were shortlisted on our platform in April 2023. Within weeks we were able to raise more than 50 per cent of their target. We're making solid progress now and are well on our way to become a gamechanger in the healthcare innovation ecosystem, which wouldn't have been possible if I stopped knocking on doors after having so many slammed in my face in the beginning.

Every Little Detail Matters

I once made a post on LinkedIn about the differences between leading a large organization and a small startup, and received a reply that really hit home for me. The poster, a CEO of a medical robotics company, shared how he washed the dishes and wiped the conference tables after everyone had left for the day.

'It's . . . a great reminder that each has a role and all of them matter. We all have to share in the responsibility for the presentation and performance of the company. None of us is truly above another,' he wrote.

His words perfectly encapsulate the differences between running a startup and helming a large organization. In the former, every detail matters. You're building a company from the ground up and hopefully creating a culture that will stand the test of time. If you allow unsavoury habits to root, it'll define your organization for years to come. An MNC already has systems and processes in place that you follow. Even less capable individuals won't dramatically affect an organization, thanks to the solid foundation in place.

I'm a lot more hands-on now compared to before. Previously, I had a big team that handled the preparations. All I had to do was turn up at a meeting and talk. Now, I help to organize events and ensure that everything is just the way it needs to be. I can't just delegate the work. That's not the mark of a servant leader. I have to help with execution and go into specific details for the team to follow.

In the past, I was more selective of the people I met for work. I received so many invitations that it became difficult to accept all of them, and most didn't amount to anything substantial. Now, I explore all sorts of opportunities, big or small. I say yes to almost everything and go in with an open mind, understanding that all it takes is that one big break to really push our company to the next level.

One characteristic that's common for large corporations and growing startups is motivated employees. They are an important component for success. In corporations, I used to encourage my staff through promotions, overseas attachments and larger-than-expected increments and bonuses. Startups usually can't offer the same pecuniary benefits. So, to motivate my staff, I started an Employee Share Option Plan at the start of 2023.

It was something that had been on my mind since I started VentureBlick. I've always envisioned the company to be owned not just by me, but by all our employees and eventually by the broader medical community.

We've all heard a lot of stories about startups becoming huge successes, but only a few founding members of these companies end up financially successful. I believe this should not only benefit a few founders. Many people actually take the risk and contribute to the growth of the company at the early stage. They should also be rewarded. I set aside a significant portion of VentureBlick for this purpose. So far, every single full-time employee who is currently with us has been granted share options. Beyond motivation, my hope is that it will foster a greater sense of belonging and ownership within the team.

I'm still a student in this classroom called entrepreneurship and she's a hard, but fair, taskmaster. Like life, business gives you the tests first, then the lessons after. I've survived several rounds and I expect many more challenges in the months and years to come.

Success doesn't come easy. But nothing worthwhile in life ever does.

* * *

Questions to Ponder Over

1. If you could do anything in life without fear of failure, what would you build?
2. What is stopping you from building that dream besides failure?

Chapter Eleven

The Beginning and the End

I don't wear a shirt anymore to the office unless there's an important meeting with an external party. The chair, too, is definitely not a Herman Miller. I'm not complaining. It's comfortable enough, but prods me to build VentureBlick into a roaring success.

I have a confession. I ploughed my life savings into this startup. It's a significant amount—eight digits long with multiple zeros and commas—and more than enough for me to retire and lead a life of leisure. But, I knew that life wasn't for me. I've always enjoyed building something and for over four decades, I built several subsidiaries and organizations. However, none of them were me. It was always at the behest of others. Now, I'm finally building something for myself.

There were the detractors. A few have said that I'm too old to start something new, others have shared that a healthcare-focused startup like VentureBlick is challenging due to the regulatory hurdles and several believe that I just don't have the hunger I used to have when I was younger.

I don't take their comments to heart. And to be objective, some of their remarks make sense. Entrepreneurship is seen as a young person's arena because of the long hours and back-breaking work one needs to put in. Therefore, youth and vitality are, dare I say, prerequisites in building a business. These are characteristics that a younger person will usually have in abundance.

Ironically, though, I've always felt that the older generation are more suited to entrepreneurship. We bring with us a large Rolodex of contacts that we can call on, garnered a wealth of experience that will benefit the startup, and more importantly, shown our spirit and can-do attitude despite our advanced age. For the young, failure just means rolling the dice again, whether in the corporate world or starting another business. For entrepreneurs like me, we cannot fail. That means we have to be incredibly confident in the business' prospects.

And I am optimistic in VentureBlick's future. I've already assembled my leadership team across the globe, stretching from Australia to Europe. I call them my 'Avengers' and I'm 'Nick Fury', sans eye patch and cool ship.

I've also learned several things about human nature—both wonderful and unsavoury. People's attitudes change when they learn that you're working in a startup as opposed to a multinational company. When I was leading divisions at the latter, many were friendly to me, picking up my calls and replying to my messages without fail. Yet, I sensed their disingenuousness beneath their smiles.

I was right.

When I started VentureBlick, they ignored me. Some even pretended to not know me. I don't like it. My personality and attitude has remained the same; only the title has changed. These incidents remind me to be consistent and respectful to everyone no matter who they are or where they work.

On the flipside, though, I've also experienced incalculable warmth, kindness and professional courtesy. People whom I've worked with in the past, but have lost contact as time erodes those bonds, reached out when they heard about my new venture. Some have wished me good luck, others offer assistance if and when I need it and a few have even asked to join the adventure.

I am grateful to them.

* * *

VentureBlick almost didn't get off the ground.

When I started the company, I also went for an annual health check-up. I was expecting a clean bill of health. I felt completely fine; in fact, I rarely see the doctor for medical reasons. Instead, I received a serious phone call a few days after the check-up from the medical professional who said I needed to urgently come in.

I went to the clinic, still thinking this was just a routine appointment. Instead, the doctor had the black-and-white scans of my brain on the wall with several squiggles and a few circles. He pointed to one of the circles and said, 'Chris, this is the left part of your brain and there is a line there that looks like a tumour. It's growing to the right side.'

I asked the doctor what it meant and what my options were. With nary a single tremor in his voice, he told me that there was a chance I could die. 'There is a slim possibility that it could develop into blood cancer. I would put it between 3 and 4 per cent now. But, I can get rid of it.'

Getting rid of it meant going for surgery, which involved surgeons using a laser to remove the growth in my brain. I was in the hospital for a few days to recover and went back to work immediately after.

I felt calm throughout this process. I understand why people panic. The jolt upon receiving such grave news can drive people to the precipice. When I told one of my earliest hires—she had followed me from my previous company—she worried immensely and told me she couldn't sleep. I shared with her that if I'm unbothered by it, then she should feel the same way, too.

In this leadership journey, I've learned to control my emotions. I also pride myself on my resilience. The best leaders have both qualities in spades.

I once posted several photos of myself with VentureBlick's different country teams and one person commented that I should smile more; I rarely break into a grin or a frown and maintain a neutral expression. My years in management have taught me that your staff will interpret your facial expressions to discern the fortunes of the company. So it's best to remain poker-faced.

Remaining calm comes from resilience. I attribute this to my decades of taekwondo training. I practised daily from when I was three years old to the age of twenty, and while I no longer work on it, the lessons from that period still remain. When you're resilient, you can withstand almost anything life throws at you. And life will come at you fast the higher you rise in your corporate career or the bigger your startup grows. If I wasn't resilient, I wouldn't have carried on when I had my health scare.

* * *

As a leader, while you're responsible for the company's direction and fortunes, your people execute your vision. They must believe in it.

When I first conceptualized VentureBlick, I wanted to build the foundation using blockchain. Because of the battering the technology has received, I changed the ship's sails. But its direction remains the same—value-adding to the healthcare industry, which I strongly believe needs change. And I hope to be the one to effect it.

VentureBlick embodies all the leadership, management and business lessons I've learned in my past thirty years that I've encapsulated in this book you're reading now. My dream is to build a company that can stand the test of time and colleagues and employees can be proud of.

Ray Kroc only began building McDonald's when he was fifty-two. Colonel Sanders was even older—sixty-two—when he began franchising his fried chicken restaurant. Leo Goodwin started automotive insurance giant Geico (Government Employees Insurance Company) with his wife when he was fifty. There are several more examples like these littered throughout history, of older entrepreneurs who still had a lot more to give to the world.

The name Chris Lee is well-known in the medical and healthcare industry for achieving stellar business results. With VentureBlick, I hope my name will be spoken about in the same breath as Ray Kroc, Colonel Sanders and Leo Goodwin.

People ask me, 'Why are you doing this?' I'm not just doing this for my own financial gain and goals. I want the people who believed in me enough to join my venture to be more successful than when they first joined. My aim is to be remembered as a good people leader with the attitude of an 'Asian Maverick'. In the broader scheme of things, I want to play a more impactful role in the healthcare ecosystem and change lives with innovative solutions.

It's ambitious, but the world is never changed by reasonable people. It's transformed by mavericks.

Chapter Twelve

Reflections

In many ways, this book reflects my current goal—entrepreneurship in service of a greater good. I began consolidating my experiences, anecdotes, and thoughts for *The Asian Maverick* at the same time I founded VentureBlick. I started the latter because I wanted to prove that age is no barrier to entrepreneurship and to help medtech startups with shallow pockets, but deep ambitions, achieve their goals. This book, too, has similar visions. I wanted to complete my trilogy—I've written two books previously—and hope to push Asians in the corporate world to achieve their own leadership aspirations.

There is no better time than now for Asians to reach the upper echelons of large organizations. There are already several who climbed to the top and, in the process, inspired many that ethnicity shouldn't be a barrier to success. Satya Nadella took twenty-two years to reach the top of Microsoft after joining the company as a young engineer in 1992. He became the company's third CEO after the inimitable Bill Gates and Steve Ballmer and has slowly grown the tech behemoth year after year when it looked like it was losing steam under the latter.

Another Asian recently thrust into the limelight is TikTok CEO, Chew Shou Zi, who testified before the US House

Energy and Commerce Committee in 2023 and shed light on the social media app's data collection and privacy practices. His poise under fire charmed those watching and multiple positive memes were made around him.

And what about Jensen Huang Jen-Hsun, the rainmaker at Nvidia? The billionaire co-founded the software company at thirty and has overseen the chipmaker's growth from scrappy start-up to technology giant. The company is now at the cutting edge of AI and deep learning, thanks to its chips.

I might not breathe the same air as these giants, but it's possible that this book might inspire someone, perhaps even you, to become the next Asian maverick. I spent close to a year writing the words you're reading now while juggling my entrepreneurial responsibilities. It was a tough slog. I have an absurd amount of respect now for writers who do this day in and day out. Looking at financial statements is more my cup of tea.

Still, it was a great exercise for me. Time and age have a way of blurring memories and burying ideas. Putting this tome evoked these long-forgotten souvenirs of an eventful corporate life that has given me much joy. In the process, I also reconnected with several characters from my past as I did research for my own anecdotes, just to make sure I wasn't misremembering them. We've made plans to catch up the next time I'm in their ports.

I once had a teacher who told my class, 'Even if I impact only one of you in this lesson, I don't see it as just one person. I see it as one generation.'

If this book only influences one person to become the Asian maverick the world sorely needs, I don't see it as just one person. I, too, see it as one generation.